AGENTS
OF
CHANGE

UNLEASHING THE INNOVATION OF REAL-LIFE SUPERHEROES

MIKE THOMAS

MIKE THOMAS

DEDICATIONS

This book is dedicated to my amazing wife, Lisa, for encouraging and supporting me as I pursued this crazy adventure. None of the examples, the ideas, or the stories found in these pages would have been possible without your love and support, and I am beyond lucky to have found a partner who has stuck with me through it all.

Thanks also to our 3 Super Kids, Mara, Aaron, and Lana, who have brought me so much joy and who remind me constantly the true purpose of my life.

CONTENTS

Introduction: Agents of CHANGE

Part 1: Super Powered Innovation

Part 2: A Culture of Super Empowerment

Part 3: Discovering Our Super Purpose

INTRODUCTION:

AGENTS OF CHANGE

We all have a superhero with us... waiting to be unleashed. As humans, it is our nature to want to make a meaningful impact on this planet, to touch the lives of those around us, and to leave behind a lasting legacy. **We yearn to be an agent of change.** We are fortunate to live in a time where technology has super-charged our ability to create, to communicate, and to collaborate, giving us more tools and gadgets in our utility belts than at any time in history. But these technological superpowers have come with a price, as they have also filled our lives with clutter and with craziness. We want to put on our capes and to unleash our super potential, but we too often can't escape the chaos within our own phone booths.

My inspiration for *Agents of CHANGE* is to celebrate these real-life super-heroes, to identify some of the *kryptonite* that gets in our way, and to help enable that untapped superpower potential. As I translate this superhero idea from the pages of comic books into the real world, a role that epitomizes this concept is that of the Innovator. As a profession, Innovators take on challenges like searching for the elusive cure to a devastating illness, advancing how the world learns and communicates, or formulating better consumer products and services to improve day-to-day life. Their jobs are, quite literally, to change the world. And while many of the examples, stories, and metaphors in this book reference those in Innovation careers, they are intended to apply far beyond the cubicles as well. Every teacher who helps to ignite a student's passion for learning, every coach who helps stubborn players learn hardwork and sportsmanship, and every parent who navigates a minefield of temper tantrums, bullying, and first dates is as much of an Innovator as those who have that title on their business cards.

We are all tasked with solving the world's biggest (and smallest) problems, with creating magic out of the mundane, and with boldly going where no one has gone before. Our mission is to change, to improve, and to even save the lives of those around us, whether that be on a global scale, in our communities, or in our homes. On paper, the role of the Innovator should be the most exciting and awe-inspiring job on the planet. So why isn't it?

Why do we spend less energy answering the unanswerable questions and more instead answering the unmanageable email inbox? Why do we spend less time hypothesizing and debating creative solutions and approaches, and more time in mundane Monday meetings endlessly nit-picking semantics and logistics? Why do we spend less thought on charting a new course for an amazing adventure, and more on charting status reports against sometimes small, trivial progress? As superheroes, we feel destined to use our powers to take on a super mission. So why aren't these powers being unleashed?

So who am I to write this book and to take on this challenge? From a career standpoint, I have been in the "Innovation Business" for over 16 years. Over that time, I have been lucky enough to learn from some talented people and from some amazing adventures. I have had the good fortune to experience the pinnacle of success with some transformational and disruptive innovation, and also to suffer through the depths of disappointment through a monumental market failure. I have traveled to many of the richest countries in the world designing beauty products for the prestigious upper class, and have also hiked through impoverished rural villages in India, China, and Brazil attempting to find health and hygiene solutions for families surviving on less than a dollar per day. I have worked in organizational cultures that promote empowerment, freedom, and creativity, and also those that are enveloped with micro-management, risk-overtness, and fear.

While I have spent the past decade and a half in the "innovation business", my adventures *beyond* the confines of my office have shaped my views and philosophies at least as dramatically as my experiences at work. I play my far most important role as the husband to a wonderful wife and as the father to 3 remarkable kids. I am an avid sports fan and spend many evenings and weekends attending professional sporting events and coaching little league games. I also am a connoisseur of science fiction and action movies, and I particularly have an unhealthy obsession with Star Wars. By no means do I feel that the sum of these experiences have made me the pre-eminent expert on the vast topic of Innovation. I do hope, however, that some of the insights that I have gained can at least ignite a *spark* for you as you endeavor through life's innovation journey yourself.

All that said, if you are reading this in hope of a "12-Step Process" that is scientifically proven to drive incremental innovation improvements for your organization then this is not the right book for you. If you are searching for precise tools, terrific templates, or standard operating procedures to yield consistent and predictable results, again go back to the bookstore and pick up one of the many texts dedicated to these ends. Looking for a sure-fire way to become rich, famous, and powerful beyond your wildest dreams? Well, I would be sharing in that very same success if this book contained all of those answers, but sadly (for us both) this book will not be the guide on that quest.

Instead, you will discover an intentionally messy and divergent collection of metaphors, parables, and principles to help trigger how to infuse magical innovation back into our products, our organizations, our careers, and our lives. This book is divided into three parts, each comprising of a collection of snackable stories, personal examples, case studies, and fables that are designed to yield some guiding insights for winning innovation. The first part focuses on the work itself, as I present ways to re-define "Quality" to guide the delivery of Amazing and Delightful Innovation. The second part dives into the importance of a Culture of Empowerment, so as to unleash the potential and the power of our people to create an environment that supports fearlessness and risk-taking. Finally, the third part closes with ideas to help each of us uncover our own Super Powers and our Super Mission— to find our purpose and to re-ignite our passion to fuel the fire of game-changing innovation both at work and at home. It is this combination of work approach, culture, and sense of purpose that is critical to delivering Super-Charged Results.

Innovators are not just those individuals who have *Innovation* on their business cards or who have labels like "The Creatives." Innovation can happen in any walk of life, at any role by the people who are empowered to take risks, who choose to fearlessly solve the unsolvable problems, and who seek a purpose-driven adventure to change the world. Innovators truly are the modern day superheroes, and as you read this book I hope that you find something that will help you to unleash your own inner powers and to become an Agent of CHANGE.

PART I:

SUPER-POWERED

INNOVATION

"The sound and music are 50% of the entertainment in a movie."

-George Lucas

As a kid who grew up in the late 70's and early 80's, the first superheroes in my life existed a long time ago in a galaxy far, far away. I spent a good portion of my childhood wearing a black glove on one hand, wielding a lightsaber, and battling the evil Empire. And even this past Halloween, I grew a beard, donned a tunic and cloak, and played Obi-Wan Kenobi alongside my son's portrayal of Anakin Skywalker. Star Wars is more than just a passion area for me— it is a way of life.

I love the above quote from George Lucas, highlighting the importance of sound and music in a movie. With Star Wars, it is easy to think of the iconic characters, the epic space battles, and the story of the struggle between good and evil as the elements that defined the "quality" of that franchise and made it so successful. But imagine those movies without the John Williams score and that very magic fades away quickly. That musical soundtrack, designed to enhance the *experience*, can have as much weight and as much impact on the audience's overall enjoyment as the characters, the story, and the plot. That said, experience alone is not enough either. Lucas, for example, arguably took this quote too far when he made the second Star Wars trilogy years later, which, although had even better special effects and soundtrack than the original trilogy, was commonly thought to be lacking in the story and character department. In essence, no matter how much magic you can create in the overall experience, the functional benefits— in this case, the story and characters— need to be right for that magic to be activated. Performance alone or the experience alone is not enough— to produce something that is truly amazing in quality the design has to be holistic.

This lesson applies beyond movies to virtually any category of products and services out there. In the chapters that follow, this idea of designing *Amazing* into the product experience will be presented as an opportunity to rethink how we define Quality in our innovation programs today. Quality has become less about delivering a product or experience *full of* superiority, elegance, and panache, and more so synonymous with executing something that is *free from* defects, mistakes, and complexity. And while the latter definition is still critically important to insure that our products consistently provide the promised benefits, to deliver a truly amazing and even magical Quality, every element of the broader holistic proposition must be deliberately designed as well. Super Charged innovation does not just quietly and thoroughly satisfy a consumer need— it also unleashes experiential delight.

1

Re-Defining Quality

Quality. It is a term that is used frequently, particularly when discussing innovation, but one with differing definitions. On one hand, we talk of quality in the traditional sense of "it is not quantity, but quality that counts". Here we strive to create magical experiences and services, to design breakthrough product innovations, and to take bigger and bolder risks. This is the quality we expect from fine Belgian chocolates, hand-crafted Swiss watches, or an authentic Swedish massage. On the other hand, we talk of quality in the more "Six Sigma" sense of eliminating defects and of striving for perfection. In this case, quality is less about the uniqueness and superiority of the product, and more about the consistency and the lack of mistakes. This is the efficiency in the mass production of automobiles, the consistency of experience you receive in a fast-food chain, and the reliability of a website in e-Commerce sales. Essentially, one definition is about being "Amazing" and the other is about being "Perfect". Both are critically important, but often in opposition, and an organization's balance between these two interpretations will significantly impact its priorities, its culture, and its results.

In trying to find a complete definition of "quality", the best I found came from BusinessDictionary.com: "*A measure of excellence or a state of being free from defects, deficiencies, and significant variations...*" This definition represents both the degree of "excellence" element as well as the state of being "free from defects" aspect of quality discussed above. Interestingly, in this definition these two vectors are separated by an "or" and not by an "and". In practice, I do believe that this is a tension that most organizations face— is it more important that we be *amazing* or that we be *perfect?* The obvious answer is "Both", but in reality one will get priority over the other. Further, the pursuit of one will more than likely negatively impact the pursuit of the other. For example, the level of risks required to innovate something *amazing* can hinder the pursuit of *perfection*, while the degree of rigor and rules to deliver *perfection* can constrain the ability to strive for *amazing*.

A balance is crucial as both sides of the coin are important in both the short and long-term success of your business. That being said, I would argue that most organizations are putting an over-emphasis on perfecting the "state of being free from defects" rather than pursuing the riskier, more stretching innovations. As you think of your organization, what is the role of "*Quality* Assurance"? Is it on assuring quality via amazing products and experiences or is it on insuring a reduction in risks and a minimization of mistakes? This is a critical distinction and one that can dramatically impact an organization's priorities, its reward structure, and its culture. Likely, the balance of the role of Quality Assurance centers on the minimization of mistakes rather than on the pursuit of excellence. Again, this is not to trivialize that responsibility, as it is most certainly vital... but simply incomplete. Particularly as we promote mantras to our organizations such as "Quality is everyone's responsibility" and "Quality is our top priority", we need to be abundantly clear on what the definition of *quality* should be. And this definition must include not only the Strive for Perfection, but the Pursuit of Amazing as well.

As I begin the journey into this book, I have chosen to start with the topic of "Quality" because this should be the target of our endeavors when it comes to our careers, our products, our organizations, and our lives. No one would argue that the strive for Quality is critically important, but it is even more essential that we define for ourselves what exactly this Quality should entail. These first four chapters are going to focus heavily on driving quality and innovation in the workplace through the lens of product design. But while the stories and examples may predominantly focus on product development in the office, the concepts and principles apply outside the cubicles as well. In my most important job, as father to three wonderful kids, I must constantly strive to give them a Quality childhood— not just through ensuring that they are properly fed, sheltered, bathed, and cared for, but that they experience some thrilling and inspiring adventures along the journey. As we all strive to be innovative at home as well as at work, this struggle to define the balance of "Quality" between being perfect and being amazing is crucial in all aspects of life.

With the world moving at a pace that often feels out of control, and the activity / time ratio higher than it has ever been, it is critical that we are deliberate in all aspects of our jobs and our lives with how we invest our time, our effort, and our creativity. Getting clear on how we define Quality for ourselves, how we set a cultural tone that supports that definition, and how we ignite a personal passion to bring it to life are the key steps to unleashing our inner superhero and to leading amazing lives and careers.

2

The Value Equation

When all is said and done, what truly is the purpose of focusing on quality in our endeavors to deliver super-charged innovation? While important, it is certainly not merely about preventing defects, about minimizing costs, or even about maximizing efficiency. While those are all factors, these are the *trees* and not the *forest*. The true overriding goal of optimizing Quality is to maximize the Value to our consumers so as to ultimately deliver optimal Profit to our business. Period. If we can design, invent, and deliver propositions of a superior value then we will have a sustainable and profitable business. Quality is about optimizing the value equation both through maximizing *excellence* in delighting our consumers, while also minimizing costs through driving financial and organizational efficiencies. So, if quality is about driving the Value Equation, what is this equation?

Defining the Value Equation

There are many ways to define this, but in its simplest form:

$$Value = Benefit / Cost$$

Basically, the quality of our innovation can be measured by the overall ratio of the degree of consumer benefits that we provide versus the costs of providing that benefit. In this case, I would define "Benefit" as, at minimum, the degree to which a consumer need or want is satisfied. Going beyond that, delivering against an unmet need, satisfying a new *job to be done*, and delivering an amazing "Wow" experience all represent ways to exponentially increase the Benefit. The "Cost" can represent not only money, but also time, resources, effort, and complexity. Cost often is the part of the equation most associated with operational definitions of Quality Assurance today.

The trick to this equation is that Benefit and Cost are not independent variables, particularly in programs which require a stretch outside the typical innovation box. For example, the pursuit of an increase in benefits to deliver a "Wow" typically comes with an increase in Degree of Difficulty; and this Degree of Difficulty ultimately leads to an increase in costs and complexity. On the flipside, the pursuit of reductions in Cost typically comes with reductions in risk, uncertainty, and degrees of freedom; and these reductions will ultimately limit the ability to provide an increase in benefits. **Said differently, in the pursuit of Quality, a focus on Costs tends to work against Benefits, and a focus on Benefits tends to work against Costs.** Both are important; an investment in Benefits ultimately leads to greater consumer delight and an increase in sales, while an investment in Costs leads to improved efficiency and an increase in profitability. Delivering value thus results from solving this tension of both trying to increase the quality of benefits and in trying to decrease the costs. The question is—which comes first?

Which Comes First? Delighting the Consumer or Delivering Profit?

This may be the most important question of all, as the answer to which will drive the focus of not only our innovation programs, but of our organizational cultures as well. It often is argued that the fundamental purpose of a company is to deliver profit and to maximize value to its shareholders through making as much money as possible. Clearly, profit is important and a company will not continue to exist much less be successful without making money. That being said, I believe that a stated *purpose* of "maximizing profit" is fundamentally flawed, and ultimately will be destructive to the long-term success of the business. Yes, profit is critical— but it is an output and not a purpose.

Our purpose fundamentally must be to maximize consumer delight and satisfaction, with profitability as a result that flows from successful delivery of this purpose. While this may sound like semantics, I assure you that it is not. Much has been written about Steve Jobs and his approach to leading Apple as well as the legacy that he left behind. **One of the critical themes of his approach was to delight the consumers first and the shareholders second.** Essentially, first figure out how to make something "Amazing" and then figure out how to make it profitable.

If you have ever been on a Disney vacation, then you have been immersed in another great example. In a Disney theme park, the Imagineers on the design team have spared no expense in insuring that every experience, every interaction, and every detail will transport you to the "Most Magical Place on Earth". From the world-class rides, to the Princess breakfasts, to the scents and sounds being pumped through the parks, Disney has put a primary focus on driving amazing consumer delight. And, also, if you have been to these Disney experiences then you know that they have figured out how to do this in a profitable way, as they have made your ability to spend money to be magically easy as well. They focused first on the experience and second on profit, and have created a delightful and successful business.

Particularly for innovators, if profit becomes the primary objective then choices will be made to **minimize–** reducing costs, reducing complexity, and reducing risks so as to drive profit through improving the bottom line. The problem is that all of this minimizing, while potentially driving short-term profits, will ultimately also minimize the ability to deliver breakthrough, new, and superior products over the longer-term. If on the other hand, the primary focus is on consumer delight, the innovators will focus on **maximizing–** improving the consumer benefits, satisfying unmet needs, and delivering an amazing "Wow" experience. While in the short-term, this approach will likely require increased investments and thus have a negative impact on profit, in the longer-term this will ultimately serve to maximize not only growth to the top line but to the bottom line as well. This is by no means saying that our innovations should not ultimately be optimized for profitability. Rather this is to say that **we should first deliver an amazing, delightful benefit to the consumer and then maximize its profitability...** and not vice-versa.

"A business that makes nothing but money is a poor business."

-Henry Ford

And while there are clear applications of this value equation in innovating new products, this applies equally as strongly outside of the office as well. It is very easy to get caught up in over-focusing on the activities and costs of life so that we fail to fully enjoy the benefits. Do we focus too much on worrying about scrimping and saving for our retirement that we fail to invest in enjoying the moment today? Can we find ourselves working excess hours out of a fear of failure, that we miss out on taking time to enjoy our successes? Do we try too hard to fill our children's time with accomplishments and resume builders for a better future, that we compromise their simple pleasures of playing, laughing, and exploring in the present?

Whether at work or at home, as you and your organization focus on quality, how much time is spent working on the numerator (Benefit) versus working on the denominator (Cost)? Typically, I would argue, that a disproportionate amount of time is spent on minimizing Cost. This is largely because it is easier to both dimensionalize and to measure and that, at least on paper, it is lower risk and complexity. Thus, quality programs are often focused far more on being free from "defects, deficiencies, and significant variations" and less on insuring delivery of "excellence" in innovation potential. To ultimately maximize the quality of our innovations and thus the value that we deliver, **we should broaden our scope of "Quality" to focus first on delivering superior benefits and then subsequently on superior costs.** While this investment can have short-term challenges, the long-term benefits will be dramatically enhanced.

3

First Amazing, Then Actionable

Perfect is the Enemy of Amazing. I truly believe that the quest for *perfection* can not only diminish our innovative capability, but also create a culture of fearfulness rather than fearlessness. Innovators can become more concerned with minimizing mistakes than in maximizing potential, and this *fear* will lead to safer and smaller innovations. By no means am I saying that excellent executions are not important or that we should loosen our standards on the products that we launch to consumers. It is quite the opposite, in fact. Particularly as the speed of innovation accelerates, organizations become leaner, and individuals become more distracted multi-taskers, it is more critical than ever to have robust and effective quality assurance systems in place. The question is not a matter of *if* we should emphasize minimizing mistakes, eliminating defects, and flawless executions— it is a matter of *when*.

When this emphasis of minimizing risk, punishing mistakes, and eliminating uncertainty is brought from the execution phase into the definition and invention phases of the innovation process, then more problems will be created than solved. In these early stages of innovation, a focus on minimizing risks will yield safer and smaller ideas. Punishing and tracking mistakes will lead to less experimentation, boldness, and agility. Eliminating uncertainty will lead to less disruptions, breakthroughs, and true inventions, and ultimately result in more marginal product improvements. And to make matters worse, all of this emphasis, while on paper showing improvements in measurable "quality", will ultimately diminish our ability to deliver true quality in the end. An over-emphasis on *Perfection* in the early stages of innovation will lead to smaller initiatives, and thus require more programs to deliver against financial objectives. As more projects are started, the organization will be spread thinner and initiatives will become smaller yet. And so a "cycle of doom" will begin that will not only decrease the efficiency and yield of our innovations but also, because of the over-extension of resources, will actually *increase* the probability of the quality incidents that we were attempting to avoid!

Again, this is not to say that Quality should only be a focus on the late stages of the innovation process. Rather, this is to say that while in the execution phase, quality assurance measures should be focused on *Perfection* (minimizing defects, mistakes, costs), and in the early phases these measures should focus on *Amazing* (superior products, size of prize, invention, and experimentation). This evolving definition of "Quality" throughout the process will still allow for the flawlessness of execution that we need, while insuring that what we execute is excellent and superior. Said differently, **it is far easier to take something amazing and to make it actionable than to take something actionable and to make it amazing.**

What You *Should* Do is More Important than What You *Could* Do. In our "need for speed", we are often in a hurry to jump right into execution and to move quickly through the *fuzzy* front end of definition and invention. We say things like "do the last experiment first" and "innovate with the end in mind" so as to get to a *faster* answer− but this type of approach will likely not yield a *better* answer. If our goal is truly to drive bigger, better, and fewer innovations then we need to invest the time, the money, and the people up front into defining the right problem before launching ourselves into solving it. Our quality measures should focus on insuring we have answers to the *"what"* questions before we launch into the *"how"* questions. What is the Big Idea? What is the Size of Prize? What will our Competitive Advantage be? What Points of Superiority must we have? What Points of Inferiority are Acceptable? What is Our Intellectual Property? What is the Desired Consumer Experience? If we hold ourselves to high standards in the early stages, we will insure that we will deliver the bigger, better, and fewer innovations we seek in the later stages.

An example from my life was in building a treehouse with my kids in the backyard. It was an exciting project, and there was a lot of energy to "just go buy some wood and start building". We could have quickly done some rough measurements, figured out the key safety requirements, bought some wood, and assembled a functional structure in the trees. And trust me… there was a lot of temptation to do that. But the kids, particularly my son, had a greater vision in mind and demanded that we first figure out what an amazing treehouse should be before we started to build. This 6-year old (at the time) aspiring architect drew up some blueprints with a front porch, a second floor balcony, and a creative slanted roof in the trees. He also filled in some requests for indoor plumbing, a television, and a storage room for his Legos. And while we weren't able to realize his whole vision (sadly, I'm not a plumber or an electrician), we ended up in a much better place than had we skipped right to building. Of course, in execution, we had to still do all the thoroughness in getting the right materials, insuring safety, and translating the physics of a 6-year old boy's brainstorm into the real world. And we also had to work through the nervousness and fear of trying to transform this fairy tale into a wooden structure within some pine trees. But because we allowed ourselves to dream big first, we not only ended up with a better result but one to be proud of as well. In our roles as innovators, we are often tasked with "building a treehouse". We need to dream big, plan smart, and execute with excellence to turn visions into actions into realities.

"It is not enough to do your best; you must know what to do, and then do your best"

- W Edwards Deming

Measure Twice, and Cut Once. When it comes to driving true quality on the early phases of innovation, this simple phrase is a very concise way to summarize a best practice. In our organizations, how much energy is spent on the *accuracy* of making the right cut versus the *precision* of making a perfect cut? In the pressure of trying to hit a launch date or to accelerate innovation, it can be a natural tendency to rush through the early phases so as to allow sufficient time for execution. We know that making a thorough, precise "cut" takes time, so we hurry up to start cutting (often knowing that we will need to cut more than once). At the end of the day, there often is "never enough time to measure once, but always enough time to cut twice". Our primary focus should be on a thorough, accurate measurement before we ever start to worry about making a final, precise cut.

"There is nothing so useless as doing efficiently that which should not be done at all"

— Peter Drucker

Simplifying Too Early Makes Things More Complex.
Often in an effort to accelerate innovation and to insure greater quality in execution, we can eliminate "degrees of freedom" for our innovation teams. We might limit the ingredients in a formulation, the complexity in a new process, or the uncertainty in experimentation so as to better insure success. While on the surface this may seem like a sound approach, for an innovation team this push for simplicity can actually make the process more complicated. I like to use the analogy of a "ship in a bottle" – if we ask a team to build an amazing "Ship" but constrain them to putting it into a "Bottle", we will definitely simplify scope by limiting the materials, the size, and the variables that the team can utilize for innovation. However, in adding these constraints, we will greatly increase the time and complexity to logistically complete the task. At least as much creativity and energy will be put into solving for the constraints of the bottle as will be invested in designing the details of the actual ship. Whereas had we asked the team to deliver a ship that was the size of the bottle, but not constrained them with the bottle itself, we would have ended up with a better and faster solution. Said differently, we should focus on giving our teams simple success criteria, but not simplifying constraints, allowing the team the degrees of freedom they need to complete the task.

One of my favorite real-world examples is that of the design of an EKG machine that could be cost-effective and portable for use in rural India. In a desire for speed and simplicity, the team was first given minimal degrees of freedom and asked to take an existing developed market device and to "water it down" so as to meet the design and cost needs of this developing market. Working under these constraints did not work and the team failed to deliver anything even close to the targets needed for this low-income market. They essentially ended up with a marginally cheaper, clunkier, and far less effective version of the original. This same team was then given the freedom to design it from scratch and to meet the same performance and cost success criteria, but now to do so however they best saw fit. The team very quickly delivered an inventive solution that was not only a success in India but that was ultimately reapplied in developed markets. Again, being prescriptive on the "what" but allowing freedom on the "how" ultimately yielded a better and faster solution.

"Everything should be made as simple as possible, but not simpler."

-Albert Einstein

This "First Amazing, Then Actionable" mantra is a simple yet critical operating principle that I recite nearly every day with my teams. Again, none of this is to say that quality measures should be deemphasized, but rather that the definition should be broadened so as to drive "Amazing" in the early stages and "Perfection" in the latter. Encouraging and measuring the elimination of mistakes, minimization of risks, and constraints in the latter stages of execution should complement and not replace the emphasis on experimentation, boldness, and freedom in the early stages. The broadening of this definition will not only yield more quality in the definition and invention phases, but ultimately in the execution phases as well– as the results will be bigger, better, and fewer innovations.

4

We Are What We Measure

In science, the term "Observer Effect" means that the act of observing will influence the phenomenon being observed. Basically, the observation of a system will actually impact and change that system. In a business context, a similar phenomenon is seen which can be considered the *"Measurement Effect"*. What an organization decides to measure for initiatives, teams, and individuals will directly impact the behaviors and results. Essentially, **we are what we measure.**

When done intentionally, this is a strategic and effective way to drive the behaviors and results we want and need for our business. The problem arises when our attempts to measure various aspects of our business and our people have unintended and undesirable consequences. For some extreme examples:

1) If we measure initiatives primarily on their speed to market, then we will likely end up with smaller, simpler, less unique technical solutions.

2) If we reward teams for a lack of mistakes, then teams may be less likely to take on additional work, attempt anything of risk, or to show agility or speed.

3) If we just simply measure and track too many things in a given process, teams may avoid the process altogether, focus on the wrong things, or find ways to cut corners.

4) If an individual's performance and compensation is largely derived by the sheer number of initiatives that he successfully completes, he will likely take on more and safer programs, and avoid the bigger, riskier ones.

The list can go on and on… ultimately, we must be strategic, cognizant, and deliberate about what we measure and track within our organizations. These choices will largely shape the culture, behaviors, and results of our initiatives, our teams, and our individual performers.

Do You Want to Break Less Rules? Make Less Rules. It has become so easy to generate, track, and report data on virtually every detail of every process, that we can become inundated with information. As technology continues to expand, and computing power increases exponentially, our ability to measure a variety of details increases each and every year. In an effort to manage the uncertainty and complexity, often organizations will enact more and more quality measures in order to control the outcome and to minimize risk. The intent, of course, is sound and often involves logical solutions to the growing amount of information. The challenge is that the increase in the number of rules can not only bog down the process but also cause individuals to put a lower emphasis and awareness on the more important rules in order to satisfy the sometimes overwhelming quantity of less important ones. The solution— we must remember that just because we *can* track it doesn't mean that we *should*. We need to get clear on the handful of rules that are truly important and track those, emphasizing the ones that are the most critical drivers of the process. This will not only drive efficiency in the system, but also will ultimately increase accuracy and quality as individuals will emphasize following the important rules rather than wasting time worrying about breaking some unimportant ones.

Celebrate "Web Gems" more than a "Lack of Errors". I am a lifelong baseball fan and have always been a nerd for all of the statistics of the game. As such, I am a huge fan of the book, *Moneyball*, a true story of how the evaluation and prediction of player and team performance is being revolutionized by new statistics and measures. There are many direct reapplications to the business world and one that is relevant here is in the assessment of defensive players. Historically, the top measure for evaluating the performance of a defensive player was Fielding Percentage. This percentage is calculated as the percentage of balls hit to a player (called "chances") that were expected to be outs, of which were actually converted to outs. While this statistic can be informative, it is highly incomplete and potentially misleading. For example, this statistic does not account for a player's range (i.e. his ability to increase his number of chances). The fielding range of the most talented shortstop may produce significantly more chances per season than an average shortstop, and because these chances are often more risky then there can be an increased chance for errors. So, this more talented shortstop may have a lower fielding percentage than the average shortstop, while actually making more plays and preventing more runs due to his increased range. Taken to an extreme, if a shortstop truly wanted to maximize his fielding percentage, he would avoid difficult plays altogether and focus on executing the simple plays with excellence. While this would positively impact his fielding percentage, the team would suffer as more runs would score for the opposing team. So instead of evaluating defensive players based on lack of errors, teams are now assessing performance based upon the number of runs prevented from scoring (which factors into consideration the exceptional shortstop's ability to successfully execute plays that the average shortstop cannot). ESPN has a segment known as "Web Gems" in which they recognize the top plays on a given night and track them throughout the season. These are the Amazing plays that, over the course of a season, can serve to highlight who the truly outstanding defensive players are. As we track individual performance in our organizations, we should focus less on tracking the minimization of errors, and more on tracking "Web Gems".

Factor in "Degree of Difficulty" when evaluating performance. To keep with the sports analogies, one concept from Gymnastics which can be reapplied to organizations is the assessment of "Degree of Difficulty". While a gymnast ultimately is evaluated for her execution, she can obtain a higher total score based upon the level of challenge for her particular routine. The riskier and more complicated the routine, the higher the potential score. As we evaluate the performance of individuals in our organizations, are we assessing them merely on how often they *nail the landing or* are we also considering the degree of difficulty for their *routine?* During annual performance reviews, are individuals rewarded for the consistency of *results* or for the *behaviors* in taking on the biggest challenges? It is critical that Degree of Difficulty be considered in assignment planning and performance reviews, not only to reward individuals for taking on a greater challenge, but also to encourage the entire organization to work on the biggest rather than the most initiatives. In the end, we should reward those who enable *Bigger, Better, and Fewer,* and not just those who just deliver *More, More, More.*

Be Clear on Points of Superiority, Points of Parity, and Points of Inferiority. Finally, I want to share an example of how being very clear on our initiative success measures can have a dramatic impact on the final result. Developing superior products is a goal for most innovative organizations, and a key challenge that many of us face. Even within this goal, we must be careful to be crystal clear on our definition of superiority so as to ultimately guide the right behaviors and results. Do you remember when the first Blackberry Smartphones started to make their ways into the business world? For me, this is an extremely memorable event as it revolutionized how I did my work. Suddenly, my email, calendar, and phone were all literally in the palm of my hand and I had much more flexibility in how and when I worked than ever before. At the time, not everyone in the organization had one so there was a "status" element to these as well— so much so that some individuals (who will remain nameless) were actually going so far as to "accidentally drop" their current phones so as to get upgraded to a new Blackberry. This really was a remarkable device at the time, which enabled more freedom and flexibility than ever before. That being said, if you break down the actual performance elements of the device, it left a lot to be desired. The phone quality was terrible, as it was very difficult to have a consistent conversation without poor sound quality and dropped calls. The calendar was highly clunky and actually created a ton of errors in syncing across devices. And then there was the email… the typing was so difficult and inconsistent, that you wanted to insure that "Sent from my Blackberry Device" appeared at the end of the email so that others knew that the gibberish you sent was due to the phone and not the product of your own idiocy! Yes, overall this product offered superior benefits through not only the unique combination of features, but more importantly through changing the way that business communication took place. However, for the main functions of the device (phone, email, and calendar) the device was actually inferior to existing, competitive options. So the question is— would your organization have launched this highly successful product with these points of inferiority or would it have waited until each vector was parity or better to competition? Even for something as simple conceptually in the big picture as developing superior products, we must be careful that our smaller picture measures are specifically tailored to enable the overall success. This may include defining not only points of superiority, but also points of parity, and even acceptable points of inferiority in the quest for developing superior products.

To conclude, these first four chapters represent a challenge to more broadly think about our definitions of Quality. This is by no means to say that we should no longer work to deliver Perfect executions. Clearly, there is nothing more important than the consumer getting a safe, consistent product that is made both as intended and cost-effective to the business. Our challenge is to insure that as we define Quality it is not merely about the absence of mistakes, but also about the delivery of Amazing. The same rigor that is placed upon perfection at execution should be carried into the definition and invention phases as well. However, rather than focusing on minimizing mistakes, defects, and risks, we should focus on maximizing benefits, experiences, and possibilities. Quality is and should be the job of each and every one of us, and is more than merely delivering quantity without errors. We should broaden this definition so as to drive overall value both to the consumer and to the business through focusing on "First Amazing... Then Actionable" with the right measures to support it.

5

A Rose by another Name Actually Does Not Smell as Sweet

With all due respect to Sir William, I have to say that he got this one wrong. Sure, technically a rose gives the same olfactory experience no matter what it is called. There obviously is nothing about changing the name of an object that also physically alters that object. That said, a change in name does alter a person's *expectation* and thus affects how that person experiences the object. For example, I enjoy drinking Sprite and like everything about the carbonation and the sweet citrus flavor. However, I once picked up a glass of clear liquid that I thought was water and then took a drink to find Sprite instead. I nearly choked, and was surprised and negatively impacted by an experience that didn't match my expectation. It was the same Sprite that I have always enjoyed and that would show no difference in a technical analysis or a blind taste test. However, it was different to me because it fit into a different context in my mind.

I heard an example several years ago that has stuck with me and really illustrates this point. A research team placed a consumer study on chocolate pudding and gave three different pudding prototypes to three distinct groups of people to assess which was the most "chocolate-y". One group received a pudding sample that was light, almost tan in color, the next group a sample that was a medium, typical brown, and the final group a pudding that had a dark, rich almost black color. The study showed that the ratings of flavor correlated directly with the color of the pudding— the darker the color, the more *chocolate-y* the pudding. As you may have guessed, each pudding actually had the exact same flavor and differed only in color. All differences were driven 100% by the color and the perception that each represented. The truly amazing twist in this example? Not only were all of the puddings the same flavor— the flavor was actually *vanilla*! Not a single panelist noticed that the pudding was not even chocolate at all. It looked like chocolate and was named chocolate, so the panelists tasted chocolate. I love this story as it very clearly illustrates that design elements, which we sometimes take for granted because they aren't driving *real* performance, can actually have a dramatic impact on a person's *perception* of performance. Perception truly is reality and it is imperative that we consider this in designing our products, our services, and our experiences.

Instead of merely delivering *performance*, deliver "A Performance". As I said in the introduction to this Part, Star Wars is a great example. The epic struggle of good vs. evil. The flawed characters who transformed into heroes. The amazing space battles, new worlds, and plot twists (Luke... I am your father). All of these of course were the *heart* of what made Star Wars great. But the soundtrack— the fanfare at the beginning, the thematic music that moved the stories and characters along, the very last celebratory notes to close the trilogy, brought the *soul*— the magic that truly created an epic experience. An iPhone camera would work just fine if it didn't make the camera "click", but that click makes it feel more like a real camera. Dandruff shampoos don't need to "tingle" on your scalp, but that is a powerful signal that the product is working. As we design our innovations, it is more than just driving a functional benefit– it is about composing a holistic experience.

Focus on the whole journey, not just the destination. Most products that we use and make are designed to deliver some sort of end benefit. We want clothes that are clean, cars that take us from point A to point B, and food that quenches our appetite. However, our enjoyment of the end benefit is almost always more driven by the experience in using the product than by the actual end benefit itself. You can get clean teeth without a minty flavor, but it is less refreshing. A Harley doesn't need to have that distinctive engine roar, but it makes the whole ride more enjoyable. One of my favorite examples involves the initial invention of instant cake mixes. The design team found a way to make a mix in which you could "just add water" and bake it. Lab tests and blind testing showed that the cake tasted at least as good as *real* cakes made from scratch, and the design team was sure that they had an obvious success on their hands. The team gave the mixes to a bunch of moms, and asked them to try the product and to evaluate it. Consistently, the moms rejected the product. Baffled, the researchers asked "why?" Was it the taste of the product? Were the directions too confusing? No– the moms had no problem with the end result, but rather with the process. No longer did they feel the satisfaction from actually *baking* and they felt less of a sense of fulfillment in doing something to delight their families. What was missing? These moms thought that they should at least need to crack some eggs and add them to the mix. This one simple step, while technically unnecessary and actually adding time and complexity, turned out to be critical to the experience of baking. And so the designers added the technically unnecessary step of "Crack 2 Eggs" back into the process, and instant cake mixes became an instant success. As we think of our own products, what are the *cracked eggs* in our journeys that may not seem important on the surface, but ultimately are critical to the overall satisfaction with the destination?

Make Design a part of the process from the start and not just at the end. There often is a temptation in doing product design to get the real, functional performance elements done first and then to add the "fluffy", experiential design elements in later. Essentially, first make it work and then make it look pretty at the end. This is a huge missed opportunity, and innovation is much better served if design elements and design thinking are deliberately incorporated at the onset. Even in projects that are on the very front end of innovation where it is tempting to lock ourselves in the lab and to focus on the technical details, we can benefit from having Design involved from the start. Often we can deliver performance benefits that are noticeable in lab testing or among the team, but can be missed by our consumers. While our projects may be our top focus for 40 hours per week, for our consumers these products provide just one out of hundreds of experiences that occur for them on a given day. Design can help direct consumers to our new benefits through intentionally integrating signals and cues that emphasize performance. What should "clean" smell like? What should "fast" sound like? What does "healthy" taste like? We should put as much energy into designing in the signals and cues of performance as we do to the technical nitty-gritty from the onset of our programs.

If you go home on Valentine's Day and tell your significant other that you brought her a dozen "skunks" or you give her a bouquet of black roses, she will not enjoy the aromatic benefits of the roses you bought (And your Valentine's Day will probably *stink*). In designing our products, services, and experiences, *everything* matters and we should focus on each element of the entire journey. Make your product epic, and compose a symphony of impactful and memorable delight.

6

The Domino Effect

"Did we actually face our critics and reinvent our pizza from the crust up? Oh Yes We Did!" In 2009, Domino's made a dramatic, bold, and risky move, with a product and commercial reinvention of their iconic and market-leading pizzas. The product upgrade itself was impressive as they transformed what had been an inferior product to a competitive, if not superior, pizza. More impressive, however, was in how they presented the upgrade commercially. In a nutshell (*in a pizza crust?*), their advertising message was:

- We have listened to our customers and now recognize that our pizza has become inferior

- We are embarrassed and this is unacceptable

- We apologize and are committed to making it better

- Our pizza experts have designed and engineered a far better pizza

---

• We are so confident that our new pizza is better that we challenged even our harshest critics to test it for themselves... and we won!

The resulting market turnaround was practically instant (in 30 minutes or less?!) and totally reinvigorated sales and the equity of the brand. The most impressive part of the story, however, was how Domino's chose to acknowledge and to face their problems head on, and to humbly address their critics. Instead of shying away from their deficiencies and focusing on their new innovation, they first publically and personally faced the music. They even went so far as to admit and to present their biggest complaints such as "Your crust tastes like cardboard" and "Your sauce is like catsup". And while this was a bold move *externally*, I can only imagine how challenging this conversation was *internally*. Before they could even begin to execute this plan commercially, the entire organization had to stop pointing fingers, hold hands, and work together to change their product, their strategy, and their culture. They had to accept that the business model that had made them successful, "Faster, Cheaper, but not Better" pizza was no longer successful, and that they needed a new approach in order to win in the evolving competitive landscape. They had to take accountability that the product that they had worked together to develop and sell was now failing to delight their customers and inferior to their competitors' offerings. They had to acknowledge that they needed to change, urgently and united.

I admire this story, not just for the success of the innovation on the business but more so for the courage of the entire organization to recognize, to accept, and to execute the change that needed to be made. Domino's approach to innovation highlights many of the principles around re-defining quality and holistic design from the previous chapters, and also provides insights on not only the consumer-facing obstacles to innovation but some of internal organizational challenges as well. How often do organizations, particularly those with a history of market leadership and success, fail to see the writing on the wall, either because they aren't looking for it or because they refuse to accept it? How many organizational cultures will support a truthful and pragmatic assessment that "Our competitors have surpassed us and we need to change course?" without killing the messenger? How many teams can get past the "That's not how we do it here" to a "How we do it here no longer works so we need to change"? Domino's is a great example of an organization that culturally, strategically, and innovatively made a bold change to save their business before it was too late. How can other organizations initiate their own "Domino Effect" to establish, maintain, or re-establish product superiority?

1) Listen to your Customers. This one probably does and should seem obvious, but is a critically important and frequently underestimated first step. First and foremost, we are designing products and services for someone else to use, so we must understand what is delighting and disappointing our consumers. In the case of Domino's, it is not as if suddenly their pizza crust started to "taste like cardboard" with sauce that "tasted like catsup"– this is something that many of their current and past consumers had been saying for years. It was only when the business results started to truly suffer that they began to accept this as a reality that needed to be addressed. In our businesses, what are the points of inferiority that may have been acceptable when we launched, but over time have become a consumer dissatisfier and/or competitive disadvantage? Whether through consumer research, reading consumer comments and complaints, or even shopping with and visiting the homes of our consumers, we must actively listen for areas of dissatisfaction (or potential new areas of delight) so as to proactively adapt and improve our offerings.

2) Know Thy Competition. Particularly when working from a spot of market leadership, it is critical to remain constantly aware and alert of who your competition is and what they are doing. Who are your top competitors today and what are their strengths, weaknesses, opportunities, and threats? Who will be your competitors tomorrow— both the smaller players in your current industry growing via "niche" positioning and/or distinctive new benefits as well as new players from adjacent industries who potentially can change the rules of the game (e.g. Apple's impact on Sony and the music industry)? Personally use their products, talk to your consumers about them, and benchmark their performance head-to-head with yours. Study their intellectual property, understand their business model, and analyze their cost structure. Have a strong respect and pragmatic assessment for your competition today, predict where they will go tomorrow, and determine what you need to do now and into the future to maintain or obtain a competitive advantage.

3) *Humbly* and *Honestly* admit when there is a problem. Before an organization can focus on fixing a problem, it must first admit and accept that there is one to be fixed. Having regular two-way communication with consumers and rigorously studying and testing the competition are key *activities*, necessary to understand and to dimensionalize any problems that may exist. More important than "collecting the data", however, is supporting and encouraging a culture that demands and rewards honest and open communication of real, unfiltered "bad news". Don't kill the messenger— reward him. If consumer research shows that our marketing message isn't working, don't rationalize it— repair it. If technical testing illustrates that our product is being out-performed, don't "spin" the data— learn from it. If an organizational culture and reward structure is such that it punishes failure and hides bad news, then it will be virtually impossible for an organization to realize, much less react to a critical gap in performance. In order to promote a culture of open communication, each individual must feel safe, secure, and even rewarded for humbly and honestly uncovering and sharing real-time data, especially when it is bad.

4) Invest in winning. So you know that you are losing, so what do you do now? Again, this is an easy answer in principle, but often far more complex in practice— if you are losing today, then you must invest in winning tomorrow. Conceptually, no one will disagree on this point, but often this simple and obvious approach will cause dramatic shifts in strategies, goals, and success criteria. Particularly if you are coming from a position of market leadership, it is likely that much of the technical organization has been focused on and rewarded for measures such as scale improvements, cost savings, and profit margin enhancements. All of these are of course critical to the long-term success of the business, and especially valuable and appropriate when you own both market leadership *and* product superiority. However, when losing market share, especially due to product inferiority, the focus must shift to investing in the product and re-growing market share. In the case of Domino's, they had grown on a platform of speed and cost-effectiveness, without necessarily focusing on the quality of the product. "Cheap and fast" tends to be easier to copy than "good", and as competition closed the gap, they did so with superior product offerings. In our own organizations, we need to insure that our strategies and our measures reflect the realities of our position. When we are winning we can focus on cost-savings and efficiency, but **when we are losing we must invest in superiority.**

5) Prove It. Once Domino's improved their product, they ran an independent study showing that they were now actually preferred (3 out of 5) in a blind taste test to Papa John's and other leading competitors. Running this study effectively "put their money where their mouth was" showing their consumers, their competitors, and their critics that not only had they invested in superiority— they had achieved it. Again, it is important to not underestimate this step. In placing this study, there was a risk of generating *bad data* that could have shown that they had failed to meet their goals. By having the confidence to place this study, they not only proved *externally* that their work had paid off, but also proved *internally* that the cultural shift had been effective. When responding to a business crisis that is the result of an acknowledgment of losing, there is no better way to turn the tide than to generate and promote data highlighting that the new strategy is now winning. This step will help the organization to put the past behind them, to celebrate in the present, and to boldly and fearlessly march into the future.

6) Remain vigilant, agile, and innovative. Once all of the *dominos have fallen* and success has been achieved, an organization cannot stop there. It must set up the dominos and do it all over again. This "domino effect" is not an event— it is a process. The reality of the moment will be fleeting as consumer desires and competitive offerings will change continuously, necessitating constant monitoring, adjustments, and evolution. Once a successful dramatic transformation has occurred, the organization must now insure culturally and structurally that they are prepared to fight to maintain that superiority. Successful results are an important landmark of success and proof that a strategy is working. The critical element though in maintaining that success is through continuing, developing, and rewarding the behaviors of vigilance and agility to promote an enduring *culture of winning.*

7

Raiders of the Lost "R"… Putting the "R" back in "R&D"

Indiana Jones has to be one of the most innovative movie heroes of all time. By day, a nerdy college professor, but by night a swashbuckling, archaeologist adventurer! Of the four Indiana Jones films, the third one is by far my favorite— Indiana Jones and the Last Crusade. In this film, not only does Harrison Ford reprise his role as the adventurous professor, but Sean Connery also joins the cast as his less daring, but more studious, father. Han Solo and James Bond in a movie together— who could ask for more? As the movie begins, the heroes are literally on the quest for the Holy Grail and the path is predictably treacherous. Not only is the grail hidden in a secret and mysterious location but the location itself is guarded by a series of lethal traps and obstacles. Many had tried to reach the grail, but none had succeeded—nor had they lived to tell their stories.

When Indiana Jones and his father ultimately find the hidden location of the Grail, they learn that there are four deadly challenges standing in the way of their completing the epic quest. And while the Joneses possess as much courage, creativity, and resources as anyone, these are not the assets that ultimately allowed them to achieve that which so many other previously had failed to do. No, it was not the adventurer persona that primarily saved them, but rather that of the nerdy professor. The fundamental reason that no one else had been able to *keep up with the Joneses* was the quality and the quantity of the *research* that they had done. Particularly the elder Jones had studied the grail for years, which gave them the competitive advantage that they needed to acquire the treasure that they sought.

Clearly, Indiana Jones needed his courage and creativity to step forward and to attempt to conquer the deadly challenges, but he did not need to step forward blindly. Because of the years of study, driven by his father's intellect, passion, and thoroughness, Indiana Jones possessed all of the tools he needed to successfully navigate the treacherous obstacles.

Knowledge: The thorough understanding of the Grail through years of studying, researching, and experiencing allowed Jones to step knowingly through the first challenge without (literally) losing his head.

Data: The accumulation of data, through experimentation and the testing of hypotheses allowed Indiana to successfully take the right path through a complicated maze where one false step would have been fatal.

Wisdom: Faced with a seemingly insurmountable chasm, Jones's wisdom gained from the research allowed him to take the correct "leap of faith" and to cross a boundary that no one else had been able to cross.

Insight: To ultimately get the Holy Grail, Indiana Jones had to choose the correct cup from a selection of dozens of choices. The right choice would result in a successful completion of his quest, and the wrong one would lead to an excruciating demise. Jones had no knowledge or data to tell him which cup to choose, but through all of his research he had gained *insight* into what the answer should be, and this insight allowed him to "Choose wisely" and to successfully complete his quest.

Sure, he had his legendary fedora hat, whip, and quick wit, but the true factor which allowed Indiana Jones to succeed was the quality of his research more so than his courage and agility. Before barreling madly into their Last Crusade, the Joneses invested the time, energy, and focus to fully appreciate the challenge in front of them. The R&D role should be very much like the job of Indiana Jones— on the quest for data, knowledge, wisdom, and insight to find some magical object, product, or idea.

In today's highly competitive world everyone is on a quest for a "Holy Grail" and is in a fervent race to find it first. Organizations put their best teams against the challenge and they are investing immense time and energy into developing breakthrough and amazing innovation. This quest requires a culture of risk-taking, fearlessness, and urgency, and a team willing to march forward with the adventurer's spirit. However, in our hurry to rapidly start the development and to jump headfirst into the adventure, we must not skip the research that will ultimately drive success. The *need for speed* is often leading even the best teams to pouring all of their energy into the execution of the adventure, rather than on charting the course to first insure the quality of the design. We need to first play the part of the studious and nerdy professor so as to enable the fearless, swashbuckling adventurer.

This is not to say that we should abandon our adventures and *only* bury ourselves in our labs and our textbooks, but rather that we should invest fully in the "R" before running top speed into the "D".

Why the investment in the "R" is not only important, but is critical:

Ideas are easy, Insights are hard. We all have no shortage of ideas... our cubicles are overflowing with clever, interesting, and inspiring ideas that have the potential to win with consumers, to drive the business, and even to change the world. So if that is true, then why aren't we winning? In our excitement to bring a new idea to life, we often allow impatience or pressure to force us to jump straight to the execution. We focus on quick solutions that only touch the tip of the iceberg, but do not fully appreciate or realize the depth of the opportunity that lies beneath the surface. Even if we spend time talking with consumers, studying research data, and evaluating trends, our analysis often remains at the surface and does not fully delve into the depths of the concepts and the true motivations of our consumers. Henry Ford's quote is still my favorite here, "If I had asked consumers what they wanted, they would have said *faster horses*". We all know that our consumers want to get from point A to point B faster, but are we working to "make their horses run faster" or are we working on an automobile?

Better is boring, Amazing is awesome. None of us want "B's" on our report cards, and we all want "A's" to hang on our refrigerators. Yet we often find ourselves settling for programs that are better but boring rather than amazing and awesome. We often fail to allow ourselves the time and research to determine the truly awe-inspiring solution to a problem because we fear investing the time, money, and resources to bring it to life. So then we instead start with something actionable and try to creatively and agilely transform, through sheer will, this simpler and executable solution into something that might ultimately win in the minds and hearts of our consumers. It is far harder to take something actionable and make it amazing than to take something amazing and make it actionable. We therefore must allow ourselves the discipline to at least define what the "Holy Grail" might be before constraining ourselves with current realities.

Don't just execute with excellence... execute something amazing with excellence. Obviously, executional excellence is critical and we must insure that what we cook up in the labs can accurately, efficiently, and consistently be delivered into the hands of our consumers. We don't sell ideas, we sell executions— therefore we must put the rigor and dedication into getting it right. That said, we need to insure that the prioritization of being on time and accurate does not override the focus on being insightful, delightful, and a "Wow". Particularly in Research & Development, while we ultimately need to execute our programs, we must first insure that we research and design the right programs, and must be vigilant in insuring that before we start executing something with excellence, that that *something* is excellent itself.

Again, the point here is not that we should all tone down our adventurous and aggressive approach, and instead only bury ourselves in our books and in our labs. It's quite the contrary in fact. Our R&D and overall Innovation approach should be a fast & furious ride as we engage in the difficult and perilous quest for the "Holy Grail". However, in the quest for the Grail, we must remember that no matter how much we want it or how hard we work, we must first develop the Knowledge, Data, Wisdom, and Insights to guide us on our quests. There will be many obstacles and pitfalls along the way, as well as the temptation to settle for the easier and faster path. Are we allowing ourselves the true upfront investment in truly researching the path to be taken so as to avoid the treacherous pitfalls before us, or are we impatiently multi-tasking our way into a booby trap that will keep us from ever completing our quest? We have the boldness to take on the adventure, but do we have the patience to do the homework? To truly unleash the spirit of Indiana Jones and to find our Holy Grail, we must make sure that we insist on putting the "R" back in R&D.

8

How Does Luck Play into Successful Innovation?

Over the years, I have spent a lot of time thinking about the role of luck in the innovation process. Luck can be a polarizing word and is often preceded by words such as *dumb* or *blind*, but I tend to think of luck more positively as an unexpected, surprising, or unplanned turn of events. Looking back at the history of many major innovations, despite all of the brilliant experiments and standardized processes, the end result was often still at least somewhat attributed to luck. Comments like, "we were lucky we ran that extra experiment", "fortunately, we launched at the right time", or "we thought we had made a mistake but then something amazing happened" are commonly found in the stories of breakthrough products. Often there were a variety of successful companies simultaneously working on the same ideas with teams that, on paper, had the same skills, but one had an amazing success while all the rest were left with monumental failures. Was it merely a matter of luck and good fortune, and if so where does this luck come from?

There are several classic stories that reveal some major innovations that happened somewhat serendipitously.

Chocolate Chip Cookies: Ruth Graves Wakefield was the owner of the Toll House Inn and famous for her homemade cookies. One day, she ran out of baker's chocolate so she improvised and tossed in some chunks of semi-sweet chocolate that had been given to her by Andrew Nestle. The chocolate failed to melt in the cookies and the rest, as they say, is history. She ended up with the first batch of chocolate chips and the first ever chocolate chip cookies. The cookies became an instant classic at the inn, and Nestle gave her a lifetime supply of chocolate in exchange for her cookie recipe. Nestle then successfully launched the first Toll House Semi-Sweet Chocolate Morsels in 1939.

Kleenex Facial Tissues: In 1926, the head of Research & Development at Kimberly Clark (K-C) was a severe hay fever sufferer and was responsible for the company's Kleenex brand disposable cold cream removal cloths. He began using the cloths as a "disposable handkerchief" and was impressed by the benefit that the product provided. At the same time, researchers at K-C were becoming intrigued by the number of letters they were getting from consumers saying that they were using the product for the same purpose. They ran a quick research study and placed advertisements in a Peoria, Illinois newspaper highlighting the now two possible uses of Kleenex— cold cream removal and disposable handkerchiefs. The results showed that over 60% of responders were using Kleenex for blowing their nose and K-C correspondingly changed how they were advertising the product. By 1930, sales had doubled and Kleenex remains the world's top facial tissue.

Ivory Soap: Ivory Soap had been a key product in driving Procter & Gamble's early success as a soap and candle company. In early 1878, P&G launched an upgraded soap known as "white soap" as an effective and affordable product to delight their consumers. Several months after launch, a researcher responsible for making the soap forgot to turn off a machine when he went off to lunch, and when he came back the batch of soap was "puffed-up and frothy." The soap technically still worked as effectively as before and was shipped out into market. Consumers instantly noticed that the soap now floated and began demanding more soap with that "benefit". When leaders at P&G discovered the source of the anomaly, they decided to take the researcher's mistake, which essentially was extra air in the soap mixture, and to intentionally make it part of the product. This became a key part of their commercialization strategy and the floating soap became a top driver of the company's success.

Is there an element of luck in each of these stories? Of course— all of these examples included some form of accidental discovery that brought them to life. That being said, in each story, the key leaders made choices either to enable or to leverage this "luck" to make it successful. Wakefield had to be willing to improvise with her chocolate chips and Nestle also had to invest in this new idea. Kimberly-Clark had to pay attention to the letters from consumers and to choose to reposition a product that had already been successful. P&G could have discarded the batch from the start, fired the researcher, or fixed the floating soap rather than leverage it. In each example, someone made a conscious choice to turn mistakes or accidents into a new idea. But for each of these stories, there are millions of examples where an amazing lucky occurrence happened and was either ignored or even punished. So what are some principles so that we can be the teams with the horseshoes and rabbits' feet rather than the ones with black cats and broken mirrors?

Hire some gamblers and give them some chips. It is somewhat easy to say that if we want to create more luck in our innovation process, that we should hire some successful "gamblers". Innovative organizations are usually good at hiring risk-takers who have the passion and capability to push the envelope, and who can accept that losing from time-to-time is inherent in taking chances. But when we bring these "gamblers" into our organizations, do we entrust them with "chips", give them some time, and set them free in our "casinos", or do we micro-manage their spending, their time, and their bets? It is one thing to hire the gamblers, but if we want them to hit the jackpot, we have to give them the freedom to gamble as they see fit.

If you want to make more shots, you need to take more shots. Michael Jordan is arguably the best basketball player ever to take the court and has more than a whole highlight reel of game-winning shots. However, for every one of these shots he made, he missed several more and actually made far less than 50% of the game-winners that he attempted! So did MJ stop shooting? No, of course not— instead of focusing on the shots he missed, he focused on the ones he made, resulting in one of the most successful careers in NBA history. He once was quoted as saying, "I've missed more than 9,000 shots in my career. I've lost almost 300 games. 26 times, I've been trusted to take the game winning shot and missed. I've failed over and over and over again in my life. And that is why I succeed." Amazing innovations do happen, and rarely may they even happen on the first shot. But for truly amazing accomplishments, there are typically a series of failures for every success.

Expect to win with every bet, and don't give up with every loss. If you are in a culture that punishes failure and only rewards successes, that values only results but not experimentation, or that demands perfection over striving for *amazing*, then "luck" often is squeezed out of the equation. If, however, taking risks, challenging paradigms, and accepting (and even encouraging) failure is an accepted part of culture, then individuals will inherently place more bets. And more bets lead to more wins.

Take time to walk around the "forest" and don't focus too early on the "trees". Often, teams will try to optimize their probability for success by narrowing scope early in the innovation process. On the surface, defining the box early may appear to simplify via driving focus and minimizing choices. In reality, closing off degrees of freedom too early often adds limitations and makes work more challenging. In fact, having too intense of a focus on a specific objective is actually prohibitive to bringing in new insights and in finding lucky discoveries. Google has utilized a successful concept of "20% Projects" where they have allowed employees 20% of their time to innovate on ideas outside their day job. At one point they estimated that 50% of their initiatives came from these projects. If you want to find a lucky discovery, you need to spend some time with stimuli and with people outside of your specific objective so as to bring in fresh ideas and new perspectives.

There will always be an element of luck and serendipity in the innovation process, and that is part of the excitement of the innovation career... and in life in general. The fallacy is that this luck is entirely out of our control and cannot be influenced or exercised. We can make our own luck by bringing in gamblers, by taking more shots, and by accepting that in taking these chances that we sometimes will lose. In the examples above with Nestle, Kimberly Clark, and Procter & Gamble, the lucky stories are intriguing, but a truly amazing fact is that each of these companies is still going strong a century later. Clearly they have found a way to have "luck on their sides" in a repeatable and consistent manner. A willingness to evolve our own definitions of "Quality" as we learn from that extra experiment, to incorporate some tangential insight, or to find positives where others see negatives can help us to find that extra bit of luck that can turn something mediocre into something magical.

9

The Poker Game of Innovation

It only seems fitting to transition from a chapter on Luck to one on Playing Poker. Over the course of my career, the poker metaphor has come up repeatedly in discussions with my teams... not at all surprising when working with innovative minds and risk-taking spirits. The game of poker is a now infrequent passion of mine, and I have been playing in some capacity since I was in high school. I actually still maintain an annual game with some of these same high school friends over 20 years later. I also have played in some low-stakes card games at local casinos and in Vegas, but these have been more like the "Spring Training" of Poker rather than the "World Series". Over the years, I have definitely won more than I have lost, and used to joke with my wife that this hobby would one day pay for our kids' college educations (I'm nothing if not an optimist). Now while I may never be in a position to quit my job and become a professional card shark, I do believe that there are several lessons learned at the poker table that can be reapplied in the office. Every day, in the high stakes game of Innovation, we make choices about which "hands" to play, about how much to invest in a given hand, and about which hands that we should sit out. To quote Kenny Rogers from "The Gambler", *"You've got to know when to hold 'em, Know when to fold 'em, Know when to walk away, Know when to run"*. Getting this balance right is key to maximizing the odds of success.

The goal is not to win the MOST pots, but to win the RIGHT ones. Particularly if you pride yourself on being a risk-taker, if you always see the glass as "half full", and if you see the potential in every situation no matter how bleak, it is critical that you maintain the discipline to not play every hand. Statistically speaking, the more hands that you play, the more you will win... and also the more you will lose. There is no prize for winning the most hands in and of themselves, but rather for ending up with the most money at the end. If you dilute your bets by playing every hand, you likely will not have the time, the capacity, or the resources to invest big on the big pots. It is important to take risks, but the right risks— bet big on the "Quality" pots where the odds are in your favor and the stakes are high. Choosing which hands not to play is at least as important as choosing which ones to play.

With the right pot and the right cards, be willing to go "All In". While it is important to be choiceful, don't be conservative. When you get dealt the right hand and the stakes are high, be ready to throw everything you have against it. Heroes are born, fortunes are made, and legends are formed, when a person or a team leans in, risks it all, and wins big. One big hand can and will overwhelm dozens of small ones and often dictates who ultimately has the biggest stack of chips at the end.

Be willing to walk away from a hand if the situation changes, no matter how invested you are. We have all been in situations where something looked like a *sure thing* at the start, but then fell apart as more cards began to fall. Particularly at work, I have seen countless examples of projects that started with huge potential and investment, but through some unforeseen technical challenge, a change in market dynamics, unexpected data, etc. that potential disintegrated over time. In these situations, it is excruciatingly hard to walk away from the table, because we are attached to the pot that we expected to win and the memory of the good cards that we had at the start. A sunk cost is a sunk cost, and you must be willing to cut your losses if the cards turn against you. Throwing more money against a pot just to justify the previous investment is a sure-fire way to go home with empty pockets. There is often a fear that walking away (or running!) is a sign of weakness or of invalidating the good work that happened early in the hand. It is entirely possible to make the right decision to bet big at the beginning and then to also make the right decision to "fold big" later on— we must be willing to adapt and to reassess as each card changes and to accept that sometimes we must FOLD so that we can live to play another day.

Treat your chips as a finite resource and don't play as if you can keep going to the bank for more. When I have gone to Vegas, I have always made a conscious effort to decide on an amount of money that I am willing to *invest* and then to lock my credit cards in my hotel safe. If we play as if we have a blank check, we are more likely to bet big at the wrong times and to be less discriminating with our time and our money. Knowing that there is a finite number of chips to be played, we are more likely to invest our time, mind power, and money against the high potential hands, and to sit out the rest.

Know your competition as well as you know yourself. Poker is a game played against multiple opponents, and their choices will greatly impact your odds of winning no matter how good your cards might be. When the person across the table bets big, you need to know whether she only bets against a sure thing, bets recklessly, or bets unpredictably. Often we make innovation choices based upon what our competition has done or upon what we believe that they will do next. If we don't know our competition's history, tendencies, and risk-profiles, we are leaving results up to chance. We need to know them inside and out so that when they act, we know whether to bet, to raise, or to fold.

No matter how well you play, and how good the odds are, be willing to accept that sometimes you will still lose. You might be dealt amazing cards, do everything right, and still manage to lose to some statistical improbability. In cards, in innovation, and in life, there are no guarantees of success, and you must be willing to accept that you might lose... and lose big. Over the course of a career, if you play the game the right way you should end up ahead, but you have to acknowledge and accept that some days you will go home empty-handed. I've been dealt a Four-of-a-Kind and lost to a Straight Flush— and while that is awful luck I can assure you that the next time I have Four-of-a-Kind I will bet big again. When you gamble, by definition, you will win some and you will lose some. You need to accept this fact and be ready to come back to the table and play another hand. The only way to never lose is to never play.

Putting logic aside... Sometimes, you still should play your hunches. Every so often, I will get dealt a hand that looks bleak statistically but that I have a "good feeling" about. In these cases, where instinct, experience, and energy pull you in a direction contrary to the logic and odds of a situation, you should not be afraid to stay in the hand long enough to see if the hunch pays off. This should not apply to every hunch, mind you, but to those rare ones in which you can't necessarily explain why you should keep playing but know in your gut that you should. For me, the most successful project that I ever launched was the result of one of these hunches. I did not go "All in" from the beginning, but stayed in the game long enough for the right cards to fall and for the pot to get big enough that I ultimately invested heavily and won. Again, these should be the exception to the rule, but often our subconscious knows more than our conscious mind can comprehend and we should follow our instincts long enough to see how it plays out.

At work and in life, every choice that we make about how we spend our time, our effort, and our resources is a gamble. We only have so many chips that we can play, and how we choose to invest (and to not invest) those chips will dictate our ultimate success, happiness, and fulfillment. When we sit down at our various tables, we need to make sure that we don't recklessly play too many hands, but also that we don't unwittingly sit out the wrong ones. We need to be vigilant as the cards fall, agile as the circumstances change, and bold in our holding, raising, and folding, so that we can ultimately win the crazy game of poker.

10

Bring the Tiger into the Room

I went on a Disney Cruise several years back, and attended a talk on Innovation (yes, I am "that guy" who attends presentations while on a cruise ship in the Caribbean). There were a lot of fascinating stories and insights, but the one that most stuck with me was the story of Joe Rohde, an Imagineer and real life superhero, who was determined that Disney should build a live animal theme park. Rohde first pitched the idea with CEO-at-the-time, Michael Eisner, and his leadership team— and the idea was shot down. "Disney doesn't do zoos" was the general consensus from the team, and Rohde walked away unsuccessful.

Undeterred, Rohde returned a second time, this time armed with an incredible presentation, charts, and data and he made a compelling case for why Disney should start this new "Animal Kingdom". The pitch generated a lot of conversation and debate, but at the end of the meeting Eisner again rejected the proposal citing something to the effect of "Live animals just don't capture the 'magic' that people expect from Disney".

Again, Rohde left the meeting discouraged but just as resolved that this idea was still a winner and that he needed to bring it to life. So Rohde went back a third time, but this time he went without any slides, charts, or reports. This time, he brought a 6-Foot Bengal Tiger into the room and watched the room go from 'shock' to 'awe', as child-like wonder crossed the faces of the executives in the room. The moment was "magical", the Animal Kingdom project was approved, and the park has been a successful endeavor for the Walt Disney Company.

The point here, of course, is not literally to bring a tiger into the board room (although I have had a couple of Monday morning meetings where I could have used one!), but rather to remember the power of prototyping and "making it real". How much time is wasted in an average week, debating hypotheticals and possibilities? We can easily spend endless energy arguing hypotheses, shooting holes in others' points of view, and stalling on decisions to move forward when the substance of the conversation is solely conceptual. Taking the time to translate a concept into even a rough prototype can make a world of difference in driving real progress.

It brings it to life for THEM. A colleague once told me that I was having trouble selling in a new idea to a team because I was seeing "rainbows", when they were seeing in "black & white". Translating the rainbow in our minds into a tangible prototype can help bring possibilities in our minds to life for others and to drive consensus.

It brings it to life for OURSELVES. To carry the metaphor further, sometimes the "rainbow", when real, may not have a pot of gold at the end of it. Maybe what seemed amazing in our minds is not as compelling or actionable when prototyped. Maybe there is a fatal flaw in the thinking that can be uncovered early before developmental work is done. Even better, maybe the art of prototyping will strengthen the initial concept and better bring the whole idea to life. Regardless, early prototyping helps not only communicate the idea to others, but also strengthens it for ourselves.

Move from a hypothetical debate to a tangible discussion, and turn a war of passionate opinions into productive, pragmatic deliberations. If there are 10 people in a room, there will be 10 different mental pictures of how an idea could come to life– a prototype can help make sure that everyone is having the same conversation about the same opportunity.

If a picture is worth a thousand words, then a prototype is worth a thousand ideas. To be clear, when I say "prototypes", these don't necessarily need to be professional, functional, and proven– just a way to tangibly turn a concept into a reality. One of my favorite examples is the initial prototyping of the computer mouse. When Steve Jobs and Apple first brought the mouse idea to life, they used guitar wire, wheels from a toy train, and jar lids– clearly not an actionable product in itself– but this 'scrappy' effort brought the concept to life in such a way as to sell the idea and to stimulate technology development. Taking the time to make it real helps the discussions to go beyond ideas into actions, forces debates to go from abstract to tangible, and enables decisions to go from hypothetical to concrete.

I use this example to close out Part I, because it not only brings to life all of the key concepts but also sets the stage for the rest of the book. Rohde did his homework, knew that he had a quality insight and idea, and created a clear and inspiring vision. When he encountered initial resistance, he went "All in" and put all of his chips on the table to turn his dream into a reality. Ultimately, by bringing a tiger into the board room he created a working prototype so that everyone could see, assess, and ultimately align on a path forward that ultimately enabled his vision, his research, and his insight to be executed in reality. And while his amazing innovation was a key component of Animal Kingdom's ultimate success, it was the empowering culture of Eisner's leadership team and Rohde's own personal passion that ultimately propelled the whole proposition forward.

Re-define quality, gain knowledge and insights, and go "All in"– Turn dreams into a reality and Bring the Tiger into the Room!

PART II:

A CULTURE OF SUPER EMPOWERMENT

"The best executive is the one who has sense enough to pick good men to do what he wants done, and self-restraint enough to keep from meddling with them while they do it."

-Theodore Roosevelt

Empowerment is a funny thing. As managers, we hire the most talented, hard-working, creative people that we can, and we know that they want autonomy, authority, and the opportunity to shine. We also know that our own workloads are overwhelming, that we yearn to pull ourselves out of the weeds, and that our own growth and satisfaction would increase if we were to successfully empower our people. Yet, a vast number of employees feel micro-managed and stifled by their bosses, while the bosses themselves feel bogged down with details and unable to carve out crucial time to be strategic. If you can relate to this either from the employee's perspective, the boss's perspective, or both, then why is it that the Empowerment that we all desire can be so elusive to obtain?

This Part of the book will explore not only the benefits but also the outright criticality of an empowered organizational culture in driving innovation.

Throughout my career the initiatives which have been most successful are those delivered by a small, empowered team. It is often said that "Culture eats Strategy for Lunch" and I strongly believe that to be true. Everyone wants to be a superhero, and there is no greater superpower that can be unleashed against an innovative problem than a hungry, talented team who is empowered to control their own destiny.

11

The Power of Empowerment

One of my favorite questions to ask successful innovators is, "Can you tell me about your best experience as part of an innovation team?" Almost unanimously, the story goes something like this:

"We were a small, empowered, under-the radar team, and nobody thought our project was going to be successful. We were scrappy and creative about making prototypes and getting data, and were free to learn and to experiment. When we emerged with a winning proposition, we shocked everyone... and the program went on to be more successful than other higher-profile and highly-scrutinized programs."

One thing that is typically absent from these stories is the role of "management". The stories don't consist of examples like, "Thankfully my boss was willing to get in the trenches with us" or "Those weekly in-depth management reviews were the key to our success." The stories are absent of statements like, "Whenever we reached a disagreement within the team, we went to our bosses and they solved it for us" or "Thankfully, my manager narrowed the scope early so we didn't waste time exploring risky, out-of-the box ideas." No— if anything, the role of management was "Thankfully, our management trusted us and left us alone so that we could actually get something done!"

When looking at the above story from the innovation team's perspective, it is easy to nod our heads and say "Hallelujah! If all programs worked like that we would have a much more successful innovation culture and far better results." But, how does this look from the perspective of management? For the most part, managers shared these same experiences back when they were working on teams and understand the inherent benefits. However, it is much harder to let go of control and to relinquish the reins when actually in the management seat as the one *accountable*, but not *responsible* for the results. Particularly in times of business crisis, managers often feel more pressure to be seen outwardly as "leaders"— to tighten their grip on the program and to play a more active role in the day-to-day operations of the team. It is far more difficult as managers to relinquish that control and to trust the teams than it is to micro-manage and "protect" them.

So what then is the role of *management* in driving an innovative culture? Put simply, management's role is to make sure that the best team is on the field, that the players are given all the tools they need to succeed, and that the team has a clear goal for which to strive. From there, the manager should do his/her best to trust the team and then get out of the way. In some ways, this is counter-intuitive— that this "absence" can be a sign of strong leadership as it feels more passive than active. However, it is critical, particularly in times of crisis, that management relinquish control rather than tighten their grip. This is not an easy task— it takes active discipline, trust, and clearly defined goals and strategies. It requires managers not to lead the "rebellion" and be a part of the team experience that we all loved as innovators, but rather to enable it and guide it. Essentially, it takes an attitude of figuring out how best to serve the teams, rather than asking the teams to best serve you.

A friend and colleague compared this conundrum to the character of Lennie from "Of Mice and Men". Lennie is developmentally disabled and loves small furry animals so much that he hugs and squeezes them very tightly. Unfortunately this pressure, even in an act of love, strangles and kills them. This too can happen to our programs, to our teams, and thus to our culture if we apply too much pressure and hold on too tightly. The concept of "Culture" often gets a bad rap as being fuzzy and fun rather than functional and fruitful. This focus on culture is not about making the team *happy*, enabling good organizational survey results, or being seen as a popular manager. All of those may be side effects, but they are not the primary driver. No− the true driver is that empowered teams will always deliver better innovation and stronger results. To truly create a successful innovation culture and to lead our teams, we must EMPOWER them.

Key Elements to **EMPOWER** Innovation

Employ the right people: The only way that this concept of empowerment works is if you have a team that you can trust, that has the skills to do the job, and the willingness to lead and take risks. Invest in hiring the right people for the right roles. It is better to have no person for a role than the wrong person.

Macro manage, don't micro-manage: This is not to say to abandon the team and let them go "rogue". Get the right team, provide whatever help is needed, align on goals, and then get out of the way. One of my favorite quotes in this area is from Jim Collins's "Good to Great", "The moment you feel the need to tightly manage someone, you've made a hiring mistake. The best people don't need to be managed− Guided, taught, led− yes, but not tightly managed."

Protect the team from complexity from above: One of the most critical and under-rated active roles that you can play as a leader is to shield the team from unnecessary complexity and bureaucracy. As soon as the team feels responsibility for managing all of the uncertainty around their project, it will taint the innovation against their goal at hand. Protect the team so that they can focus on delivering Amazing results. Once "Amazing" exists, a lot of extraneous complexity becomes simpler.

Ownership delegated to the working team: The team should feel ownership and empowerment to make key decisions and recommendations to drive their programs, and not the need to always go to management for a decision. It is the leader's role to set the criteria but to push the team to make the recommendations. I often say "It is better to beg forgiveness than to ask permission".

What, not How: This is one of the simplest, yet most important concepts in empowering teams. Give the team a big, hairy, audacious goal but don't prescribe how to get there. Often, not only will the team find a way to get there on their own, but will come up with a better solution than you could have ever imagined. *"If you want to build a ship, don't drum up people together to collect wood and don't assign them tasks and work, but rather teach them to long for the endless immensity of the sea."* – Antoine de St. Exupery

Encourage rebellion, creativity and risk-taking: A team that feels challenged, inspired, and supported to do something out-of-the box, most likely will. I like the word "rebellion" here– a team with something to prove that has a strong rallying cry is most likely to do something truly new and innovative. *"Never doubt that a small group of concerned citizens can change the world. Indeed it is the only thing that ever has."* – Margaret Mead

Recognize and reward: Put your money where your mouth is. If you want innovative behaviors from your teams then measure and reward it. This means finding a way to acknowledge and reward failures, because anything truly innovative rarely succeeds on the first attempt. While results are clearly important and ultimately are the fruits of a team's labor, you must reward *behaviors* along the way to insure that the innovative push and drive persists even through failures.

For another example, I will leave the cubicles and go to a small softball diamond. Each spring, I hold the prestigious position of head coach for my oldest daughter and her girls' softball team. This has easily become one of my favorite ways to invest my time. The day-to-day working with the kids, helping them to love and to learn the game, and watching their vast improvement from the first practice to the last game is something that I have enjoyed far more than I could have imagined.

For the youngest girls in the beginner's softball league, there initially is a lot of necessary "micro-management" to not only keep the games moving, but also to protect the safety of the kids. Combine metal bats, projectiles, and the attention span of many 8-year olds, and it is easy for all sorts of chaos to ensue. In an effort to contain this "entropy" during the games, typically two or more coaches stand out in the field and help to "direct traffic". Depending on the coach, this role can range from "Lana, quit building a sand castle" to "Mara, throw it to second base!"

In my second year coaching, my coaching staff made a very conscious effort to remove ourselves from the field of play as the season went on and to empower the kids to take what they learned in practice and to own it for themselves. While this was somewhat uncomfortable and assumed a certain degree of risk, it paid huge dividends for not only the confidence of the girls but also for the results on the field as well.

The kids took accountability for the results. They encouraged each other, communicated back and forth ("Force out at 2nd Base!"), and paid far more attention than when coaches were on the field.

The girls felt far more pride in their achievements. When a brilliant play was turned on the field, it belonged solely to the girls… and the pride was contagious.

They better learned from their mistakes. When something went wrong, they had to figure it out themselves and the lessons were far more likely to stick.

Hustle increased dramatically. As they became owners of their destiny rather than blind followers of the coaches, their passion and energy grew immensely.

The coaches could step back and focus on the big picture. Instead of being "puppet-masters" for the game, we instead could think through strategy and motivation. By actively MANAGING less, we were able to COACH more… and the results improved while our own satisfaction increased.

This lesson applies to our *grown up* organizations as well, as leaders feel obligated or even pressured to micro-manage their players rather than to coach them. Particularly as pressure increases to win, it takes discipline, trust, and courage to step back and to let the players own their own destinies. While in the short-term there will be some bumps in the road, in the long-term not only will the results of the game get better, but the team will get infinitely stronger to deliver an empowered culture, a winning score, and also sustained results.

12

Would Thomas Edison Survive in Your Innovation Culture Today?

"I have not failed. I've just found 10,000 ways that won't work." This famous quote, attributed to Thomas Edison, hangs on the walls in laboratories and conference rooms of innovative companies around the world and represents an inspirational philosophy of one of the greatest innovators of all time. Edison's vision, persistence, and commitment have changed the world as we know it, and he serves as a gold standard for Research & Development and Breakthrough Invention.

That being said, if a young Thomas Edison came up in your organization today, would your culture allow him to be successful? In an environment of extreme impatience for results, multi-tasking, and internal competition, would Edison be allowed the time and budget to fail "10,000 ways" in inventing something truly breakthrough like the light bulb, or would he be weeded out through annual performance reviews? After one or two years of learning and measurable "progress" but without tangible, actionable business results, would your organization have the patience to stick with him? Would he be told to "Pick something less risky— find some low hanging fruit"? Would he suffer in performance reviews against peers with multiple low risk, low reward contributions as he strives for the high risk, high reward solution? Would he be told to "not put all of his eggs in one basket" and hedge his bets with some easier projects, diluting his time on the bolder, more challenging work? Would his managers cut his R&D budget after some initial failures, and encourage him to do the "last experiment first"? Basically, would Edison be encouraged to continue his pursuit of the light bulb, or would he be pressured to merely deliver a better candle (Longer-lasting? Scented?)?

While obviously this is an extreme example, the question is still relevant. In a world of annual, results-based performance reviews, would a young innovator in pursuit of a high risk, breakthrough invention survive in competition with peers delivering safer but actionable business results? Again, I truly believe that for organizations, "you are what you measure", and if performance reviews and promotions go to individuals who deliver safer, short-term results, then the organization as a whole will trend toward these objectives. Now, by no means am I saying that results are not important— clearly at the end of the day delivering results is what keeps us in business. However, if your objective is to be an innovation leader and to deliver breakthrough results, then there need to be mechanisms for recognizing, rewarding, and encouraging risk-taking, focus on the long-term, and even failure.

Considerations in Supporting a Culture of Breakthrough Innovation

Recognize short term behaviors and long-term results. Often organizations prioritize short-term results over everything in conducting performance reviews and in setting assignment goals. While results clearly are important, most truly innovative goals won't be fully delivered in a year (and will often take several years). If an employee's focus is solely on the short-term, he/she will often modify behaviors to compromise depth for breadth and trade off risk for *safe*. There needs to be a balance of rewarding innovative behaviors in the short-term, while evaluating actionable results in the long-term.

Redefine success and reward "smart" failures. To steal a quote from Woody Allen, *"If you're not failing every now and again, it's a sign you're not doing anything very innovative"*. Fear of failure is a key barrier in doing something truly breakthrough and individuals need to be encouraged to take risks and to push boundaries. The failures should be smart (bold but not reckless), but if innovators don't push too far then they will never know how far they can go. Reward learning, milestones, and even failures, but not merely end results.

Give credit for "degree of difficulty" in measuring performance. If you want your top innovators working against your top challenges, then you need to reward them for taking on the extra challenge and risk. With gymnastics again as a metaphor, it is much harder to 'nail the landing' on a complex, risky routine than on a basic and simple one— and this acknowledgment thus goes into the judges' evaluations. In the same manner, this degree of difficulty factor should be also enacted in innovation performance reviews to encourage top talent to push the envelope.

It is an interesting dilemma, particularly as organizations get leaner, as the need for speed increases, and as competition intensifies exponentially. Can your organization be "impatient for learning, but patient for results" and would a young Thomas Edison be successful in your culture today?

13

Remember the Processes Work for You... You Don't Work for the Processes

I will begin with a disclaimer— I am not a process-oriented individual. I am, by nature, a divergent and chaotic thinker who craves freedom and creativity in my work. I am one of those crazy people, who is comfortable at operating outside the stereotypical "box", in breaking rules (that I deem unnecessary), and in jumping out of the airplane without a parachute... confident that I will figure out a solution before I hit the ground. If you are crazy like me, then this probably sounds like an inspiring and refreshing approach to innovation. If not... well, then you probably want to lock me up in that "box" that I got out of.

It is not that I do not value processes. In fact, I am a huge supporter of any system, approach, or tool that allows me to save time, be more efficient, and simplify work. I like to push the envelope, to experiment as much as possible, and to move agilely, and so the more tools in my toolbox the better. I love processes that are designed to work for me and to make my job easier, so that I can focus on *what* breakthrough innovations that I should design and deliver and not so much on *how* I walk through the work. My problem with processes is when they are elevated in such a way that *I* am supposed to work for *them*. Statements such as "The process won't allow you to do that", or "You need to do x, y, or z to satisfy the process" drive me mad. It is as if my tool has somehow jumped out of my toolbox and suddenly become my master... and that I have now become the tool. I don't want to be a tool.

I recently had a serious office debate about what was more important to delivering successful innovation— the process or the people. To me the answer is obvious. People— no question. While processes can facilitate innovation, they are a means and not an ends. Give me any challenge, big or small, and I would rather have a small group of amazing people with no established process than a world-class process with mediocre people.

That said, I do believe that processes have an important part to play, not just in the execution of initiatives but also in the culture of an organization. When effective processes are in place for activities such as initiative management, resource allocation, and quality control *and* used to propel teams forward, then innovation can be taken to an even higher level. Basically, it is not just about having an effective tool; it is also about how you use it. Thus, a corporate culture that supports innovation is the essential element— without an atmosphere that supports some risk-taking and uncertainty, the innovators will suffocate regardless of the process. And while I completely agree that an effective process can be essential in driving ideas to reality, I also believe that over-reliance on a process can be a severe hindrance as well. When strict adherence to the process becomes more important than the realization of the invention, more harm will be done than good.

The following are four examples of how Innovation can be harmed in a world of "Processes Gone Wild":

Teams are steered to focus more on Checking Boxes than on delivering Big Ideas. When the process is in charge rather than being used as a tool, then a team can easily fall into a mode of mindlessly crossing activities off of a list rather than of mindfully looking for new ways to drive bigger and better ideas. Have you ever been in a situation where delivering against the right timeline became more important than delivering against the right proposition? If the team is truly a slave to the process, then the priority can become focused on delivering something solely Actionable rather than something Amazing and the innovative potential will be diminished.

Process outputs are treated as "decisions" rather than as "data". Have you ever had some form of this conversation, "I know that the team thinks that this is the right idea and that it has the resources to get it done, but 'The Process' says that it is impossible. Therefore, this discussion is over."? Essentially, when we work for 'the Process', then the data output can be used as an excuse to avoid hard discussions. Process data should be a resource to aid smart people to debate and to make decisions, even if the ultimate decision is contrary to what the data might suggest. As leaders and innovators, we should use data to aid in our thought process and to facilitate decision making, but not arbitrarily trust it to be a decision. Process output should not replace thought.

Teams are forced to utilize a process even when it does not add value. Processes should facilitate rather than be a mandate. For example, if an initiative management tool is designed around a 5 year innovation cycle, and a team suddenly needs to get an innovation from idea to market in 6 months, then strict adherence to that process will not be fruitful. Now, there may be principles or aspects of the process that can help steer the team forward, but most likely there will be steps and activities that need to be eliminated and skipped. If this team is mandated to use the process and to follow each step, it will lose agility, create inefficiency, and likely fail to focus on the top critical issues. Teams should be empowered to apply what is useful in helping them to complete their mission, and to exclude what is not.

Processes drive Rigidity rather than Agility. Not all projects are created equal. And more importantly, neither are all teams created equal. A one size fits all process may be beneficial from a portfolio assessment standpoint as it makes tracking initiative success, progress, and consistency easier. But from a team standpoint, a process needs to be agile enough to allow for different needs, approaches, and talents. That is not to say that there should not be any "hard points"− there are likely certain financial measures and technical proofs of principle that need to be met no matter the program. However, there also should be "soft points" that are customized based on the specific project needs as well as the team capabilities.

This is not a call to banish all processes from organizations and to let anarchy reign in the corporate world. Fun as that would be for someone like me; it is not realistic or intelligent, particularly in a large, complex, matrixed organization. The call here is to put the processes in their place− back in the toolbox. If your organization has personified or even deified a process so that individuals, teams, and even management are being held accountable to it (i.e. "We are all slaves to the process"), then that has to change. Swing the hammer and don't let the hammer swing you.

14

Busy but Bored?

It sounds like an oxymoron— how can a person be both wildly overwhelmed and insanely busy, while still being filled with an underlying sense of boredom? There is no question that everyone, particularly top performers, has more than enough work to do. In these times where competitive pressure is high, technological advances are accelerating, and businesses are being (over)stretched to do more with less, top people are not only being challenged with extra work— they are being disproportionately counted on to carry an ever-increasing workload. As managers, it is natural to look to our top people when the latest crisis-of-the-day emerges. They have proven their talent, agility, work ethic, and passion so as to be relied upon to deliver with excellence. But in doing so, are we doing a disservice not only to the individuals but to our businesses as well? What are the long-term opportunity costs in overreliance on our top innovators to carry the burden for shorter term crises? Are we empowering our innovators to invest in maximizing their impact and fulfilling their purpose or instead encumbering them by filling their minds and our calendars with activity and distraction?

This is not to say that we shouldn't challenge our top people. In fact, I am saying the exact opposite. These top innovators, without question, should be the most challenged individuals in our organizations. The trick is to insure that we provide the right kinds of challenges to the right people, and that our top innovators are working on the hardest problems. And by "hardest problems" I am not referring to the most *urgent* but rather to the most *important*. Not the highest *quantity* of deliverables but the highest *quality*. Not the biggest *workload* in our groups but the biggest *impact*. Conceptually, this sounds easy but in actuality it requires an enormous dose of discipline. As managers, there is an immense amount of pressure to focus on short-term results— and annual performance reviews, financial incentives, and resource allocations are designed accordingly. And while the challenges are real and the pressure is warranted, we need to be careful that in investing heavily in the present, we are not mortgaging the future.

Of course, we cannot ignore our short-term crises. Failure in the present may result in there ultimately being no future to support. But there must be a balance. Over-investment of our top people on crisis management and an under-investment in long-term innovation will lead to smaller and smaller programs, necessitating the initiation of more of these short-term interventions, leading to even smaller programs... and so on and so on the cycle will continue. And while the business impact of this cycle is immediate and apparent, the effect on our organization's top innovators is even further detrimental over the long-term. Ultimately, not only will these innovators likely burn out, they will also become intellectually bored along the way as they lose their own sense of purpose amidst all the noise and activity. When the puzzles to be solved become more about how to manage an over-zealous workload as opposed to solving a profound innovation challenge, the innovators will eventually tire of this cycle and seek challenges elsewhere—whether in another organization or outside their "day job". Either way, these individuals can and will not bring their best efforts into work and our organizations will pay the price. So what can we do about it? The crises and short-term challenges are not going away, so how do we insure that while this critical work is getting done it is not at the long-term expense of our innovators?

Give a man a fish and you feed him for a day. Teach a man to fish and you feed him for a lifetime. It is a natural instinct to throw our most critical and urgent challenges at our top, experienced innovators and not at our junior, inexperienced employees. It may even seem counter-intuitive to entrust these junior people with a crisis when you have battle-tested warriors at your disposal. The result of this decision—not only do your top innovators take the brunt of the crises, but your junior people miss out on opportunities to get their own battle-testing to become the warriors of tomorrow. (Not only that... these junior folks, by default, often end up leading the future innovation work that your experienced innovators ultimately yearn to do!). What if instead of this default position, we instead threw our hungry, junior innovators into the short-term fires with the coaching, but not the active engagement, of our experienced innovation leaders? While there will be some risk and apprehension for managers in this situation, the overall benefits can be profound. Your junior innovators get the battle-testing they need and the skills to grow their own mastery and leadership, while your experienced innovators get to focus on the bigger, more profound innovation problems—while teaching the future leaders as well.

Emphasize work that is not just "filling" but is "fulfilling". This one is less concrete but probably the most important of all of the points. Top people want to contribute as much as possible and will invest a vast amount of effort in helping the organization succeed. These individuals see challenges and opportunities everywhere and want to help solve as many as they can. So when they are feeling under-utilized, for whatever the reason, they will often look to fill this void by taking on extra work– essentially looking for fulfillment through quantity instead of quality. This ultimately will be detrimental not only to the organization but to the individual as well, as the excessive stretching and box checking can become the *adrenaline rush* or the *drug* to replace the seeking of true job satisfaction. Are your innovators proud of the work itself or are they substituting physical stretching of their capacity for true intellectual stretching and growth? Living on snacks, appetizers, and fast food can be filling for awhile, but in the long run serves to be very unhealthy.

Watch for signs that the work itself is no longer "reward enough". Some may disagree with me here, but in my experience, the truly sought after reward for innovators is not the money, promotion, or recognition. It is the work itself. Sure, we all want to be successful. And, yes, we want to be recognized for our work. However, we don't want to seek these things– we want them to come naturally as the effect of our doing something that we love, and of doing it well. When a talented, innovative individual starts becoming (sometimes irrationally) obsessed with a raise or a promotion, I have found that the root cause typically is an overall dissatisfaction with his/her job. The work is not rewarding them, so they are seeking this reward elsewhere. When this situation arises, try to find ways to enrich their work plans, even if you cannot enrich their pockets. What do they want to Stop, Start, and Continue doing as part of their jobs, and how can you work with them to make their day-to-day role more fulfilling? Also, are there places where you can give the gift of time or money to a side project that they might want to pursue? This investment can go a long way in driving job fulfillment, while also enabling some incremental organizational innovation as well.

Are your innovators "boldly going where no one has gone before"? Innovators want growth, and growth comes from extending into new frontiers. From a work standpoint, are we challenging our innovators to take risks and to try new approaches or are we asking them to repeatedly go from point A to point B? Beyond the work, what about our cultures? Are we supporting fearlessness or promoting fearfulness? Do our reward structures value and recognize risk taking and even failure or do they punish for mistakes. Our innovators want to take risks and to boldly pursue "impossible" problems and to make them possible, but at the same time they don't want to fail in their careers. If boldness and exploration ultimately do not support success in our organizations, then individuals likely will move away from these behaviors. I once talked to a top innovator who was working on what was, by far, the most important and challenging program in her organization. This person was fulfilled and was doing great work but the nature of it was such that there was a high probability of failure. Her management, instead of encouraging her risk taking and creative work, recommended that she take on additional, "safer" programs so as to hedge her bets. They wanted to make sure that something she worked on succeeded rather than for her to put all of her eggs in one "risky" basket. The message to her— success on something small and safe was valued more than risking failure at something big with a high degree of difficulty. The result was diluted effort on the "new frontier" work so as to work on the safer bets. While the intention was good in the short-term so as to protect and support this individual, in the long-term it ultimately led to "boredom" and dissatisfaction.

"All work and no play make Jack a dull boy..." Are our innovators enabled to take a "recess" during the day? To spend a few hours a week on a fun side project or on exploring new ideas within their existing projects? To have conversations and brainstorming with individuals outside their teams and their industries to look for new ideas and approaches? It seems that most of us are so busy that there is no longer time to stop for lunch, much less to stop and "play". Innovators love to solve problems, to try new things, and to explore new ideas. Are we supporting, encouraging, and enabling this time to play or are we focusing too much on efficiency, tracking and allocating each hour for each individual, every day? This commitment to play will, on paper, look like it dilutes work on primary objectives. In actuality it will make us much more effective. We will have a far more empowered workforce, will generate new ideas and approaches, and strengthen our current programs through renewed passion and creativity.

I ran into a colleague as I was wrapping up this chapter, who was obviously stressed and flustered, and I asked him how he was doing. He answered, "Well, I'm definitely not bored!" I honestly don't know if that was true. We often mistake activity for progress, and are in effect running so fast and furiously that we fail to realize that we are trapped in the "hamster wheel". We need to insure that our top innovators are inspired, growing, and working on our top challenges, and not just frantically stuck in the endless cycle of short-term "crises". When our *business* is over-stuffed with *busy-ness,* our culture will suffer and our innovators will become overwhelmed and underutilized.

15

Second Hand Stress

Smoking is one of those activities that clearly can go beyond the individual smoker himself to also impact those around him. Acutely, the effects of second hand smoking are tangible— seen visibly in the smoke itself, smelled on clothing, and tasted as smoke enters the body. Chronically, long-term second hand exposure can also lead to the same cancer and other diseases that impact the smoker himself.

Now, this chapter is not intended to denounce, support, or otherwise present an opinion on the habit of smoking, but rather to use it as a metaphor. Smoking is a choice that an individual can make, even in knowing that there are clear risks, through assessing that the benefits outweigh the costs. However, this choice is made more complex by the knowledge and understanding that it not only puts the individual at risk, but can also impact those around him. And this risk is easy to internalize because cigarette smoke is a tangible entity that creates a visible and observable "cloud" from the smoker outward. Essentially, it is clear and obvious for a smoker to see that his actions have the potential to have a real impact on those around him, and he therefore can (or must in many cases) adjust his actions accordingly to minimize the impact on others.

Stress on the other hand is much more difficult to dimensionalize. Similar to smoking, much of the stress that we experience in our lives is the result of choices that we, as individuals, consciously make. The late hours that we spend agonizing over a report or presentation, the time we spend writing emails on our days off, or the general over-commitments that we make in both our professional and personal lives are choices that we make to enable some personal benefit. Whether that benefit is success at work, more money to improve our quality of life, the prestige or pride that comes with being successful, or something else, we choose to take on stress as a "side effect" of our success "drug" of choice. Whether consciously or subconsciously, we decide that the personal downsides that result from stress are overcome by the upside that arises. Again, acutely there can be negative impacts— sleep deprivation, poor diet & exercise habits, anxiety, etc. can plague an individual who is overly stressed. Chronically, there are risks as well as long-term stress can be a definitive source of career burnout, heart problems, high blood pressure, susceptibility to disease, and more.

So what does this have to do with innovation or with leading an organization? As individuals, when we choose to "over work" for whatever the reason, it is easy to see that this choice can have a detrimental impact on our own effectiveness and well-being... and this may even be a tradeoff that in itself we are willing to make. What is less tangible, however, is the "invisible cloud" that emanates around us from the stress that we are "exhaling". While not tangible, visible, or tactile, the *smoke* that comes to our employees, our coworkers, and our organization is certainly real and can result in short and long-term havoc on our office culture, our innovative capability, and the overall health of our organizations.

Under stress, our strengths devolve into our weaknesses. Almost unanimously, I have found that an individual's greatest weakness stems from his/her greatest strength. If we are detail-oriented, we may turn to a micro-manager. If we are aggressive, we can get confrontational. If we are creative, we might become divergent and indecisive. What is worse, it is very difficult to recognize these behaviors in ourselves because they are so similar to the strengths that have made us successful. As leaders, it is critical that we have trusted mentors and strong partners to help us recognize both the warning signs and the ramifications of our stress behaviors. If left unaddressed, not only will our personal effectiveness suffer, but our ability to lead our organizations will suffer as well.

As a leader, our stress activities are addictive and contagious. One of my primary stress activities is to catch up on email during ridiculous hours, sometimes in the middle of the night. I often will try to remedy an over-flowing inbox by responding and forwarding email over evenings, nights, and weekends when nobody else is online. When I join a new team, this behavior is at first freeing for me as I get to feel the sensation of *catching up*, to erase some clutter from my life, and to allow myself to focus on bigger and better things. Over time, however, this behavior becomes destructive both to me and to my teams. For me, I grow to count on using my free time (or sleep time!) to commit to working, and I actually become less productive during the work day ("I will just save that for tonight when there are less distractions."). This can become a vicious cycle and ultimately I can burn out and burn some bridges with my family at home. For my group, as they get used to seeing me crank out emails at all hours of the night, they often start to believe that this practice is an expectation. The more I email at night, the more my team does as well and I no longer am just running myself into the ground... I am inadvertently running them into the ground as well. This is just one example of many, and I have no illusions that I will ever *completely* rid myself of behaviors like this. However, it is critical that these are the exception and not the rule so that my bad habit does not evolve into an addiction that is contagious.

If stress is aired out, the "smell of the place" will suffer. I spent several years early in my career working on deodorants and antiperspirants, and we used to talk about the "smell of the place". This is how we talked about the culture and *energy* of the organization. This energy or *smell* was largely dictated by how the leaders managed and communicated in times of stress. When the attitude and rhetoric was that of crisis, problems, and even panic, the organization smelled like fear. When the tonality was that of challenges, opportunities, and inspiration, the organization smelled like hope. As leaders, how we feel and respond to our own stress and crises can and will have a direct and indirect impact not just on the actions and behaviors of the organization, but on the attitude and spirit of the place as well.

An increase in pressure will ultimately decrease the volume and creativity of innovation. If you studied chemistry at all in school, you are probably familiar with the Ideal Gas Law (PV=nRT). If you did not study chemistry at all... bear with me here. Basically, for an ideal gas, if all other variables are held constant and you increase the pressure, the volume will decrease. Not only that, but ultimately the entropy (for sake of example, entropy is a measure of latent energy, randomness, and possibilities) of the system will also decrease. Taking the metaphor to this example on stress... over the long-term, if you increase the pressure on an ideal innovation organization, the volume and creativity of the innovation will ultimately diminish. Now, in the short-term, this may be masked because an increase in pressure can cause an acceleration in "activity" and maybe even some immediate progress. Over time, however, this excess pressure and stress on an organization will squeeze both the quantity and quality of work in a negative direction.

Secure your own mask first before helping others. I will admit that I have heard this spiel dozens of times from well-meaning flight attendants. Of course, I know that they are right. Pragmatically speaking I can be of more help to those around me if I help myself first. Instinctively, though, this is a difficult concept to imagine actually practicing. Most of us naturally want to help others before we take care of ourselves, particularly if these "others" are people that we care about. In our organizations, when we see our teams and our colleagues struggling we naturally want to offer our time, energy, and capacity to help them out. And to be clear, that is typically both the right instinct and the right action. However, when we ourselves are in crisis, we need to first make sure that we are under control before saving those around us. This is difficult, particularly for servant leaders, but is important to ultimately do what is best for the greater good. If we don't manage our own stress and pressure before trying to "solve the world's problems", we will ultimately do more harm than good and be less effective overall.

Clearly, much of this is an oversimplification and there are a lot of exceptions. Not all stress is self-inflicted nor is it always a negative. Sometimes situations and circumstances outside of our control lead to our overwhelmed state, and sometimes a pressure situation will actually help a team perform in the clutch. That said, the majority of the stress we live is stress we create, and over time it will take a toll not only on us as individuals, but on our organizations and our cultures. Regardless of the cause, as leaders we must be aware of the impact that our own anxiety will have and must actively work to minimize the "second hand stress" that we cause. If we descend down a path of overwork and overextension, we must remember that if we choose to poison ourselves, the air around us can become toxic as well.

16

The Lost Art of the Team

Fall is my favorite season of the year, largely because two of my most passionate pastimes are in full force and start to consume my thoughts and my free time— the National Football League and my Fantasy Football League. With regards to the *real* football, I am an avid Pittsburgh Steelers fan (despite the perils of spending my last 16 years living in rival Cincinnati), and a faithful follower of not only the team on the field but also the front office management behind their success. The Steelers possess an unmatched 6 Super Bowl titles, and have remarkably had only 7 seasons with losing records (winning percentage below 0.500) in the last 40+ years! Their trademark "Steel Curtain" defense, history of drafting of Hall of Fame calibre players, and consistency of coaching and culture have made them arguably the most successful franchise in the history of the sport.

And then there is my Fantasy Football Team. After 15 painful seasons, I have established myself as the owner of one of the most abysmal franchises in my league's history. While I like to blame bad luck, statistical anomalies, and unfortunate karma, after more than a decade of losing I think it may be time to admit that the problem rests squarely in the "front office". Regardless, I have come to expect each year that the "real" football team that I follow will have far more success than my "fantasy" team. For me, this in one case where the *reality* actually (and unfortunately) far surpasses the *fantasy*.

For those less familiar with Fantasy Football, I will provide a little background (although based on my results, I am poorly qualified!). When drafting a fantasy football team, the key is to get the best possible individual performers at all of the key positions. For example, a team with Aaron Rodgers of the Green Bay Packers at quarterback and Antonio Brown of the Pittsburgh Steelers at wide receiver would win a lot of games. In a weekly fantasy football matchup, each player is awarded points based upon his individual performance in his respective game and a team's points are a simple addition of all the players' points on the starting roster. Net, if my roster of players accumulates more points than my opponent's, then I will win the head-to-head game. So, similar to real football, the better the players perform the better the team will do. That said, there is one major difference in a *fantasy* football team versus a *real* football team. In real football, while a team depends on strong individual performances by key players, the true key to success is the collaboration and teamwork among the individuals on the team. Essentially, the individuals of a team are dependent upon each other and the results of a team can either be significantly greater or dramatically less than the "sum of its parts" based upon how the team plays *together*. In fantasy football, the result is fully based upon the performance of individuals, entirely independent of how other players perform. Players on a fantasy football team typically do not even play together in the same *real* games, so the fantasy team's results are an artifact of each individual's respective performances and are inherently equal to the sum of its parts.

So, other than highlighting the obsession that consistently impacts my focus and effectiveness in the office for three months each year, how does this all relate to the innovation workplace?

I believe that *real* innovation teams are often being designed and operated more like *fantasy* teams, and it is leading to a significant decrease in the Culture of Empowerment and thus the effectiveness and results for the business. I am often asked "What is the most dramatic change that you have seen over the past decade in the workplace?" My answer is simple— "The TEAM concept has become a lost art". This is not to say that individuals are purposefully being less collaborative or even that groups of people are failing to pursue common goals. On paper, there are still teams working against common objectives to deliver business results. But as organizations and individuals focus increasingly on "doing less with more", disproportionally rewarding multi-tasking, and working screen-to-screen rather than face-to-face, individuals are becoming less personally invested in a given team and more heavily invested in personal deliverables. For example, what once would have been a team with 5 individuals investing 100% of their time might now consist of 25 individuals investing 20% of their time. There often may be more individuals now touching a given project, each as a specialist of sorts, so as to give their input in the areas of their personal expertise. These "specialists" are now distributed across multiple programs so that they can more easily spread their contributions more broadly. Again, on paper, this looks great as projects are being done with less total man-hours, and experts are able to impact significantly more projects/person. However, in practice, what is gained in efficiency is most often lost in decreases in teamwork, accountability, and personal passion. Individuals are inherently less invested in a given project as it represents just one of many, and their focus must be on maximizing their individual contributions across their entire body of work rather than on the shared success of any given project. Teams are less empowered to take bold actions, to make hard decisions, or to change direction as they are more in a mode of execution than of innovation. While the results of all individuals, on paper, might look amazing, these results are often a *fantasy* as the lost benefits of true teamwork keep the *real* results from exceeding the sum of the respective individual parts.

This is all not to say that we should abandon striving for efficiency in our work or that we should now start being less aggressive. The *intent* behind the changes in the team approach is absolutely correct. However, the *side effect* is significant and I do believe that the pendulum has swung too far... and is getting progressively worse. As organizations strive to do "more with less", these less effective teams are instead creating initiatives that get smaller and smaller as individuals get spread thinner and thinner. Then as initiatives get smaller, more are needed and the downward cycle continues. If, however, we focus on creating smaller, more focused teams, the work will become more impassioned, teams will be more empowered and accountable, and results can improve dramatically. Then, we will not only truly deliver a *real* "more with less" but will also positively impact the organizational culture and create a positive upward cycle.

Key Attributes of a Highly Functioning TEAM

Time: This is easily the most basic concept in building effective teams, but also the most important. For a team to truly collaborate and to "row together" toward a common goal, it is crucial that individuals on the team spend actual time together. And not just in meetings and during crises—individuals who invest time and energy in building relationships, debating various points of view, and brainstorming ideas and approaches will ultimately end up with stronger innovation and better results. The most successful project and the strongest team of my career was, not coincidentally, the team that spent the most time together—brainstorming, debating, trouble-shooting, imagining, and sharing a drink (sometimes all at the same time!) This is not to say that everyone should be best friends... or even friends at all. But investing in relationships to serve as a foundation for collaboration, challenging, and creativity will exponentially elevate the performance of a team.

Empowerment: As stated previously, the most successful teams feel empowered to control their own destinies. If the individuals on a given team do not feel like they ultimately are drivers of their initiatives, but rather are "along for the ride", they will be less likely to rally together to do something amazing. An empowered team working together to bring their collective vision to life will deliver better results than a collection of individuals tasked to execute someone else's plan. Every time.

Accountability: With empowerment must come accountability, as the team must not only own the vision for the work, but must also own the responsibility for the ultimate success or failure. If an individual is measured based on how well the team as a whole produces results rather than on his/her unique contributions, it drives engagement and decision-making to elevate the performance of the broader team. "Win as a team, lose as a team, we are all in this together".

Mission: Finally, each and every member of the team should be operating against the same vision, objective, and success criteria to drive optimal performance. That does not mean that everyone always agrees. For example, Marketing and R&D can continue pushing to maximize sales and adding "bells and whistles", while Finance and Product Supply work to drive cost savings and efficiency. However, if everyone is working toward the same big picture goal, not only will the debates be more forward-thinking, the compromises around the tension points will serve to elevate the overall innovation potential of the team. Further, if the team's mission can be at least partially rooted in a personal passion for key members of the team (e.g. if a team tasked with delivering more sustainable packages is filled with avid environmentally conscious individuals), the performance will be even further heightened.

While this TEAM philosophy should seem simple in concept, it is growing further complex in practice as the need for speed, efficiency, and multi-tasking accelerates at a rapid pace. And while it may be difficult, organizations that find ways to foster a culture and organizational structure of truly collaborative, empowered, and close-knit teams will hold a significant competitive advantage.

And for me, I can only hope that the Steelers will again come together as a winning team and bring a seventh Super Bowl title back to Pittsburgh. As to my Fantasy Team... well, I guess I will just hold out for dumb luck and good karma to finally come my way.

17

Batman in the Office... Hero or Villain?

Like most kids growing up, I was a big fan of superheroes. Obviously as you read this book... I still am. Over the years though, both my taste in and definition of a "Superhero" have changed significantly. When I was young, my standard of excellence was clearly Superman. The guy was virtually indestructible, with superhuman strength, impenetrable skin, and the ability to absorb any impact without injury. He truly was the Man of Steel. In addition, he had unique and amazing superpowers, like x-ray vision, freezing breath, and of course the ability to fly. Even his one weakness was not a human weakness— it was a susceptibility to kryptonite, a rock from his home planet. He was from "out of this world"— an alien from Krypton who might have looked human, but was literally superhuman. He was my quintessential superhero, with amazing powers, unique abilities, and no human weaknesses.

Then there was Batman. To be honest, as a kid I never really saw the appeal of Batman as a superhero. The guy was strong, but he was not *super* strong, as his abilities were the result of training and hard work rather than some sort of alien or mutant ability. Many of his so-called powers did not come from internal talents like Superman's x-ray vision, but rather through cool gadgets and devices like the Batmobile, his utility belt, and a grappling gun. And worst of all, although he wore a cape he couldn't actually fly! Batman never seemed to fully embrace his superhero status, and preferred to work in the shadows— not to be the symbol of a hero always in the limelight, but rather to be an undercover hero, working behind the scenes. He was always his own boss and was willing to break society's rules, guided by his own internal principles to get the job done. Beyond that, Batman made mistakes. His temper, emotions, and risk-taking led him to make bad decisions and, while he always won in the end, it was often a bumpy ride. Essentially, where Superman was superhuman, Batman was *merely* a "super" human, in all senses of the word, still susceptible to injury, mistakes, and failure.

As I have grown up, my appreciation for Batman has also grown, and I now think that he is the most impressive of all the superheroes. Superman, for example, was destined to be a hero, with his alien abilities allowing him to accomplish things that no human could ever dream of. Batman, on the other hand, made a conscious choice to take the risk and to transform himself into a hero and do whatever was *humanly* possible to make a difference. Batman was a super innovator. He used his natural intellectual talents and invented and utilized cool tools and toys to provide himself with a unique, competitive advantage. He trained and grew his strength and skills through hard work, extreme effort, and grueling training. And most of all, Batman leveraged his passion to fight crime and to bring justice— not for personal reward or accolades, but because it needed to be done. Batman was not born a superhero— he transformed himself into one, assuming significant risks and sacrifices to do what he deemed necessary to give Gotham City the hero it desperately needed.

Our organizations need superheroes of our own. I am going to venture a guess that if I were to say "Superhero in the workforce", the majority of people would first imagine Superman and not Batman. This is the "Superhuman" who leaps tall buildings in a single bound, is the face of the organization, and who follows and enforces each of the organization's rules. This is the stereotypical *leader* who willingly takes on the role of hero and both seeks and relishes the attention and accolades that come with the role. But what about the "Batmen" and "Batwomen" of our organizations? Take a moment and think about this different type of organizational superhero who is less in the limelight, but critically important in delivering amazing results. This is the person who always gets called into the critical crises, to find creative, agile solutions to seemingly impossible problems. He or she may not be the leader on paper, but is recognized by peers as an organizational superhero. This *Batman* is not afraid to get his hands dirty, accepts and embraces the risk of failure, and is willing to break rules and orthodoxies if they get in the way. These *Batmen* will do whatever is necessary to solve a crisis and are guided by internal principles, passions, and measures of success, while far less concerned with external rules, recognition, and accolades. These *Batmen* are not driven to deliver amazing results so as to be seen as a hero, they are driven to be a hero so as to deliver amazing results.

As you think about the leaders in your organization, can you identify the *Batmen* who may not always be the face of your organization, but are often its heart and soul? Further, does your organizational culture consistently reward and respect this different type of leader, or does it actually punish and discourage them? In times of crisis, we are of course more willing to "send out the Bat Signal" and call for Batman to do whatever he deems necessary and to break any superfluous rules so as to get the job done. But when the job is done, do we continue to support this methods or do we punish his unique, principle-based approach in favor of a more established, rule-based one? Do we recognize him for his results and accomplishments, or do we criticize him for the rules that he broke and for the rebellious approach that he took? Basically, do we know the *Batmen* in our organization and does our culture embrace them as superheroes or shun them as super-villains?

The following are some common traits of *Batmen* in our organizations and some consequences for not supporting or even for punishing the principle-based *leadership from the shadows* approach that they take:

He often "Leads from the Shadows" and not from the podium. *Batman* knows that he is a hero and a leader and is not seeking external validation or recognition. He is less concerned with proving himself to his management above, but rather to support and to "rescue" the organization around him. He has a vision, a plan, and a legion of followers, but is truly a "servant leader" and is ultimately far more concerned with *real* rather than *perceived* influence and leadership.

He does not seek and even avoids credit. The reward for *Batman* is the successful completion of a mission and not the credit for his personal accomplishments. He often shies away from the limelight, feeling that his successes are "all in a day's work" and that personal recognition is unnecessary. He often will even support and promote recognition of everyone else around him… not just to deflect the attention but to further support and to serve the organization.

He doesn't ask permission… taking both risks and accountability. *Batman* has a bias toward action, and has the self-assurance to take a risk, knowing that even if something goes wrong that he will find a way to fix it. He is not paralyzed by a fear of failure but energized by the possibility of success, and trusts in himself to take action and to succeed. He will set his own success criteria, and when he is wrong (and he will be wrong sometimes), *Batman* will take full accountability both for the mistake as well as for the solution.

He breaks rules in favor of his principles. While *Batman* won't break rules for the sake of breaking rules, he also won't follow rules purely for the sake of following them. He will have very clear principles to guide his actions, but if a specific rule gets in the way of his principle-based action then he will not hesitate to break it. While he will likely recognize that there can be consequences to these broken rules, he is willing to accept them in pursuit of the big picture.

He does what is right and not what is popular. This is where *Batman* can be both heroic and dangerous. He will be very confident in his own sense of right and wrong as well as in what decisions need to be made to drive progress toward a goal. He will be less concerned with external political motivations than his internal instinctive motivations, and will thus often push in a direction off the path of the prevailing management or organizational point of view. While on one hand, this can help push through some complexity and bureaucracy to drive progress, it also can alienate him from his management or from the organization. Depending on how big the gap is between his view of "right" versus the organization's view of "popular" will dictate whether he is seen as a superhero or a supervillain.

He is always called in for a crisis. *Batman* will shine in a crisis and will likely be called in for the most critical and urgent problems and challenges. Because he does not fear failure and is accountable for his actions, he is willing to take risks to find agile solutions and to use *cool tools* that others are not able or willing to try. *Batman* will do his best work under the adrenaline rush of a crisis and will thus shine when he is needed most. However, he may struggle in "normal" business situations as he can become bored and uninspired, and because the organization may become less accepting of his rule-breaking approach when outside of a crisis.

He is better with a sidekick and mentor. *Batman* is most likely going to be extremely independent and have a difficult time in asking for help. That is not to say that he is an ineffective leader– he likely will have followers and the ability to inspire and guide others. However, when it comes to obtaining help for himself personally or to have a partner in taking risks and accountability, *Batman* will often default toward operating alone. When he does have support, though, from a *Robin* to help in balancing his passion with pragmatism and his fearlessness with caution, he can be more effective. Further, if supported by a key mentor, like Alfred the Butler, who cares for him and helps to "clean up his messes", he can maintain his freedom in being fearless in his risk-taking approach knowing that he has someone looking out for him in case issues arise. While *Batman* likely will naturally gravitate toward operating independently, if smartly paired with a sidekick and mentor his superhero effectiveness can be maximized.

While *Batman* can play a critical leadership role in an organization, he can be perceived as dangerous as well. The same comfort in taking risks, breaking rules, and taking chances that makes him "heroic" can also make him appear "villainous" if something goes wrong. An organization that properly supports these leaders and does not punish behaviors that are outside of the norm will benefit from a servant leader and hero in their organization. That is not to say that *Batman* should always fully be left to his own devices. If fearlessness turns to recklessness or independence turns to reclusiveness, then the behaviors must be coached and steered. However, if *Batman* continues to deliver strong results and is paired with the right sidekicks and mentors, then his approach should be supported and recognized. Otherwise the risk to the organization is:

- Batman will quit fighting and go back to his "cave".

- Batman will leave "Gotham" and take his fight to another organization

- Batman will become a "super villain", pushing back against his critics and causing more harm than good.

While these leaders may not fit the stereotypical view of a superhero, with their face on a billboard and their successes on their sleeves (or on their chests), they are critical to the success of an organization. So, are these leaders who lead from the shadows and are willing to take risks, to fail, and to take accountability, treated as heroes or as villains in your organizational culture?

18

The Cartwheel Effect

My oldest daughter really is an amazing kid. She is extremely clever, very graceful, and more daring than any 11-year old girl I know (if I do say so myself!). She is also entirely independent (stubbornly so) and can sometimes possess very little awareness, and frankly minimal concern, of the perceptions of those around her (I can't imagine where she gets that...). While this independent streak can be frustrating at times as her parent, I truly hope that she always maintains this spirit and continues to prioritize her own expectations and desires over those placed upon her by society.

I took some creative license with the following story, but the point holds true. Several years back, this amazing girl started to take a Gymnastics class at the YMCA. This was not a competitive program by any means, but a chance for her to exercise, to meet some kids, and to get out some of that endless supply of energy. One of the first moves that she practiced was a basic cartwheel, and one evening she came to me excited and proclaimed, "Dad, I just did a *perfect* cartwheel!" So, as the proud Dad that I am, I followed her into the basement and sat back and waited to witness perfection.

She vaulted herself forward, put her hands on the mat, and went head over heels with legs bent, flailing with a unique "twist" as she spun, in a move that vaguely resembled a cartwheel. "See Dad, I did it!" It was extremely cute and, being the ever supportive and "helpful" father and coach, I smiled, praised her effort, and offered her some advice. "Hey, kid, that was awesome, BUT... next time why don't you try and keep your legs a little straighter?" She looked at me with what I first thought was disappointment but then recognized as defiance, "Dad... my legs *were* exactly how they were supposed to be— that was a *good* cartwheel." After a short and unproductive back-and-forth, she walked away disgusted that her Dad had no concept of what a cartwheel was *supposed* to look like, and I walked away thinking she needed more practice.

Some form of this conversation happened periodically over the coming days, until eventually she stopped asking for my advice and I stopped giving it. Finally, one evening I had the "brilliant" idea (if I do say so myself) to take a video so that she could see for herself what I was trying to say. "Hey... you've probably never had a chance to actually see yourself do a cartwheel. Would you like me to take a video?" I offered slyly. "Yeah, Dad, that would be awesome!" she exclaimed with a big anticipatory grin. So she set up for a cartwheel and I whipped out my iPhone. A few seconds later, we sat together and watched the video, and for the first time she had recognition that her cartwheel was not being executed in reality as she had perceived it in her own mind. The video data showed her conclusively what I was trying to say and allowed her for the first time to internalize the feedback.

So she went back to the mat, launched herself into a cartwheel and kept her legs much straighter. "How was that, Dad?" she anxiously asked. "That was much better," I said, "that was the best cartwheel you've ever done!" Now, newly confident in my coaching abilities I decided to offer her another bit of advice, "Now, this time you can try to do it with a little less of that interesting *twist* so that you land straight ahead", I said, trying to paint a picture of my view of the perfect cartwheel. "But Dad," she said, "I am *trying* to do that twist. I don't want to do a cartwheel *exactly* like everyone else... I want to do it *my* way!" And with that, I realized a fundamental flaw in my approach. I had been focused so much on what I perceived to be the "right way" to do a cartwheel from my perspective that I never took the time to understand what she perceived the "right way" to be from hers. The communication gap was not only that her perception was failing to match up with reality, but further that *her* perception was failing to meet up with *my* perception. While I was trying to illustrate to her that her results were not matching the objectives, I failed to realize that my objectives for a "perfect cartwheel" were different than hers.

Thus the "Cartwheel Effect" was a recognition that there was a gap in:

o   My objectives versus her objectives

o   Her perception versus her own objectives

o   Her perception versus my perception, and

o   My perception versus my own objectives

This "Cartwheel Effect" extends beyond my basement, and into innovation teams and organizations. Conflicts both within teams as well as between teams and their management often arise due to misalignment in objectives and perceptions. As such, a significant detrimental effect can be seen on the Culture of Empowerment and Innovation. Managers might feel the need to micro-manage due to teams delivering against the "wrong" objectives. Teams might feel a lack of empowerment and accountability as managers' demands do not match their vision for the work. Teams can end up in an endless cycle of re-work and swirl as no one seems to ever be rowing in the same direction. To overcome this "Cartwheel Effect", teams need to communicate, collaborate, and coordinate their objectives and perceptions so as to maximize results as well as the journey in obtaining them.

Steps to Overcome the "Cartwheel Effect" and to Improve Organizational Culture:

Align on the definition of the Desired Objectives at the onset. Make sure that all teammates and managers are very clear, transparent, and aligned on the objectives of the project. While this seems obvious, it is often overlooked. At the beginning stages of a project, all key stakeholders should invest whatever time is necessary to define all of the goals and get them on paper. Have the debates and hard discussions at the start to drive focus and to minimize "swirl" moving forward. Essentially, make sure everyone had the same understanding of *why* you are attempting a "cartwheel", *who* is playing what role, and *what* a successful "cartwheel" would be.

Get clear on the measures for Project Success Criteria. Once the team has aligned on *what* a successful cartwheel should look like, they should next get clear on *how* they will measure it. "We are what we measure," and thus driving clarity on aligned criteria will help make decisions more pragmatic than emotional. Getting everyone's perceptions out in the open and assigning quantitative (or even qualitative) measures around success will be key in insuring that objectives are being broadly met.

Define "hard points" versus "soft points" for Innovation Design, particularly as the team works with their management on how to deliver against success criteria. What specific executional elements are mandated by management and which are optional, so as to give the team degrees of freedom in which to deliver the project goals? Using a hypothetical example from my daughter's case, maybe her Gymnastics coach expects a successful cartwheel to involve good form and a perfect landing, but will allow creativity in her "twist", tempo, and expressiveness. My daughter can then focus on delivering the base criteria that must be met to satisfy the Coach, while owning the creativity and agility to design and deliver in the way that she best sees fit. This will drive accountability, ownership, and creativity, ultimately leading to a better overall solution.

Make all of the various perceptions visible and tangible by "Bringing the Tiger in the Room". I've talked previously about the benefits of "bringing the tiger", i.e. taking a verbal or written debate and bringing it to life in a real way that is interactive and obvious. In the example about my daughter, we debated fruitlessly until we actually had video proof that we could both react to and thus see firsthand the previously hidden differences in our perceptions. Creating a prototype to be shared and discussed, bringing data to life with examples and metaphors, and role playing scenarios with the entire team can all surface differences in perceptions in a very real way that is far better than weeks of debates over memos, meetings, and emails.

Review the "game tape" together. As the teams learn and evolve along the journey, everyone should share the "game tapes" with each other as they move from milestone to milestone. Again, with my daughter, I could have analyzed the video in a vacuum and given her feedback through my viewpoint alone, or my daughter could have done something similar from her own perspective. By sharing and assessing the data, prototypes, and analyses together we can more easily break through each other's perceptions and more clearly align on how to proceed.

Investing the time in aligning on objectives from the start of a project, in communicating various perceptions along the way, and on actively and tangibly sharing progress and results can all help teams to overcome the "Cartwheel Effect". Until there is a shared, tangible vision for success on the horizon, then individuals on the team will ride forward in different directions and struggle along the way. As to my daughter, we both now agree that her cartwheels are beyond perfect... they are Amazing!

19

Stone Soup Innovation Culture

When this same oldest daughter was in 4th grade, their class performed a music recital, which was an incredible production of singing, dancing, instrumentation, visual arts, and more. The key theme of the show was around the story of "Stone Soup". There are several versions of this tale, but for this particular performance the story starts with three monks wandering into a village where they hoped to get a meal and some rest. As they walked through the village, they found a community of hard working individuals who largely kept to themselves and appeared generally bored and unhappy. As the monks went door to door looking for a place to stay, no one would even answer their knocks as the villagers chose to focus on their own concerns rather than to help some strangers. The monks had an immediate concern for shelter, but also saw an opportunity to rejuvenate the culture of this village. So they went to the middle of town, started a fire, and got the attention of a young girl from the village. They told the girl that they were preparing to make *stone soup*, and that all they needed was a large pot and some water.

The girl rushed home, asked her mom for a pot, and together they walked back to the monks. As the monks boiled the water, a crowd started to form as one of the monks ceremoniously placed their *magic* stones into the water. The buzz of the event spread throughout the village, and everyone dropped what they were doing to be a part of the excitement. As the monks stirred the pot, one of them smelled the soup and said aloud that it could taste even better with a dash of salt and pepper. So one of the villagers ran home and grabbed generous amounts of the spices to add to the soup. Upon adding the spices, a second monk tasted the soup and exclaimed, "What would really be delightful are some fresh carrots!" So another of the villagers ran home and grabbed several bunches of carrots. And this process continued as all of the villagers became involved, bringing meats, vegetables, sides of bread, and desserts... all to help the monks in their fascinating brew of stone soup. Upon completion of the soup, the monks dished it out and the villagers enjoyed the most delicious soup that any of them had ever tasted. Everyone laughed, enjoyed each other's company, and danced through the night, as the enjoyment of stone soup was not felt merely in their mouths and stomachs, but in their hearts and souls as well.

This story hit home for me beyond the songs and dance moves of my daughter's class, as I reflected on the role of the innovator and the leader. We often are tasked to create a delicious soup and to rally our village of coworkers to provide the effort, time, and ingredients to cook up a masterpiece. However, many times the path taken is dramatically different than that of these monks. Instead of creating an inspiring and somewhat open ended vision that attracts and enrolls followers, do we serve up a prescriptive recipe and demand strict adherence? Do we encourage a spirit of shared creativity or of strict compliance? Are we open to the amazing possibilities that the acceptance of new ideas can incite, or are we afraid of the potential chaos and uncertainty? As leaders, we want to insure that our team can successfully execute a winning recipe and to deliver the desired results on time. As innovators, we want the freedom to imagine possibilities, to experiment, and to work in a culture where all voices can be heard and new ideas can be incorporated. We all want delicious soup.

To create an environment where our innovators bring their passion, their extra effort, and their best ingredients for our soup, we need to enroll them into the process of creation higher than just the process of execution. Had the monks gone into town, told the villagers that they were making the best soup in the world, and ordered them to bring back all of the necessary ingredients, participation would have been reluctant and reticent... if it had occurred at all. As leaders, it still is important to have a bold vision to inspire and to guide the organization, but to leave that vision open enough for growth and builds from the innovative minds and spirits of the team. The beauty of "stone soup" is that it is an interesting and magical concept that inspired a community to not only be a part of it... but to invest their best time and resources to *make it better*. "Stone soup innovation" can thus not only yield the best possible soup, but an improved innovation culture as well. The monks will attract, rather than obligate, followers, the villagers will come out of their shells and openly share the best of themselves, and everyone can dance and celebrate long into the night.

20

Rebels with a Cause

As I close out these chapters on a Culture of Super Empowerment, I want to acknowledge that it was a challenge in deciding upon the over-riding theme for this Part of the book. I spent a lot of time debating whether this was really about Culture or if it was actually about Leadership. In creating a Culture of Empowerment, there inherently must be strong leadership practices in place to foster and support the right "smell of the place". While I could have gone that direction, I ultimately chose against it because the word "Leadership" tends to imply actions from atop the organizational hierarchy. It becomes seen more as a title, synonymous with "Boss" or "Management" than as an active act of courage, boldness, or guidance that can come from any individual within an organization. The Leadership that I would refer to is a "Servant Leadership" and can come from any individual at any level. A Culture of Empowerment enables, grows, and unleashes these leaders across the entire organization, and thus is a critical component of any successful innovative organization.

"Servant Leadership" is one of those terms that *should be* both aspirational and inspirational. Ken Blanchard has written much on the philosophy of servant leadership, describing it this way:

> *The servant leader feels that once the direction is clear, his or her role is to help people achieve their goals. The servant leader seeks to help people win through teaching and coaching individuals so that they can do their best. You need to listen to your people, praise them, support them and redirect them when they deviate from their goals.*
>
> *The servant leader is constantly trying to find out what his or her people need to be successful. Rather than wanting them to please him or her, they are interested in making a difference in the lives of their people and, in the process, impacting the organization. The role of the servant leader is to do anything that is necessary to help his or her people win and accomplish their goals.*

Reading this, it is hard to imagine anyone *not* aspiring to be this type of leader— a humble servant, enabler, and coach, whose sole purpose is to enable greatness for and through his organization. Yet, if that is the case then why is this leadership philosophy so rare in practice? Often, I believe that the terms "servant" and "leader" are seen as wildly contradictory forces rather than complementary assets. Leaders are strong. Servants are weak. Leaders are bold. Servants are meek. Leaders tell others what to do. Servants do as they are told. As much as I am being dramatic to make a point and intentionally writing statements with which I principally disagree, they do, on some level, ring true. If you were to do a word association exercise for the term "Leader", what would you see? I see a bold, confident, directive individual, standing in front of the room and addressing the crowd. If I were to do the same exercise for "Servant", I see a shy, introverted, passive follower, sitting in the crowd awaiting instructions from the leader. And looking around at the individuals who tend to quickly and most often climb the corporate ladder, I would surmise that in virtually every organization that "Leaders" as associated above are far more prevalent than "Servants" on the rise to the top.

So, if servant leadership as a concept is both sought after by organizations and successful in delivering results, then why is it so uncommon in practice? And, yes, it is successful. In Jim Collins's brilliant book, Good to Great, he researched companies who were able to drastically out-perform their peers for a sustained duration of time. Of the several factors he found in driving this success, one key was a type of servant leadership that he referred to as "Level 5 Leadership":

The best CEOs in our research display tremendous ambition for their company combined with the stoic will to do whatever it takes, no matter how brutal (within the bounds of the company's core values), to make the company great. Yet at the same time they display a remarkable humility about themselves, ascribing much of their own success to luck, discipline, and preparation rather than personal genius...

...Level 5 leaders are differentiated from other levels of leaders in that they have a wonderful blend of personal humility combined with extraordinary professional will. Understand that they are very ambitious; but their ambition, first and foremost, is for the company's success. They realize that the most important step they must make to become a Level 5 leader is to subjugate their ego to the company's performance. When asked for interviews, these leaders will agree only if it's about the company and not about them.

Basically, Servant Leadership works… but it is hard. It takes self-assurance, dismissing one's ego, and courage from an individual to put his/her personal ambitions aside and to do what is best for the greater good. It also takes visionary, connected, and humble management to recognize the effective servant leaders in an organization, and to support and to promote them— especially given that these individuals will likely not promote themselves. Committing to a culture of "servant leadership" is not a passive investment to boost morale and to make everyone *happier*. It is an active act of *rebellion* to serve and to protect the organization at all costs and to promote a culture of empowerment, trust, and service.

Beyond Servant Leadership— REBELS WITH A CAUSE

So, I am now making an active choice to transform my word association for "servant" into more of a bold, rebellious, and inspiring image. From now on, when I say "servant leadership", I am going to imagine Han Solo from the original Star Wars trilogy. Bear with me here. First of all, yes, I was raised on Star Wars and can probably quote every line from the movies. I grew up playing with my brothers, pretending to be heroes like Han Solo or Luke Skywalker. And now, decades later, I play similarly with my own kids (although they typically make me be Darth Vader). We cheered as these heroes served the Rebel Alliance and fought for freedom against the Evil Empire. These Rebels were willing to sacrifice everything for a cause greater than themselves, and went on to an improbable victory restoring freedom to the galaxy. Nerdy, but awesome.

Han Solo entered the story as a smuggler, out only for himself, and was more of a rebel *without* a cause than *with* one. He carried himself with a silent swagger and a sort of polished indifference that made him audacious, daring, and adventurous. As he ultimately became part of something bigger than himself, he maintained his swagger and boldness, but directed it now at the service of others. Han always did whatever was necessary to protect his friends, accepted the most daring and risky missions for the good of the team, and reluctantly accepted leadership positions granted because of his accomplishments rather than his ambition. Solo was courageous, spirited, and comfortable taking charge— and he was a servant leader and rebel.

With that new standard in mind, here are some traits of A Rebel with a Cause:

- Puts the mission above all else, always making decisions and taking action based upon the greater good of the organization and not on personal ambition or gain.

- Lives knowing that sacrifice is braver than survival and is able and willing to do what needs to be done even if personal risks are at stake.

- Uses personal humility to build individuals in the organization. The servant leader does not want his organization to ride on his coat tails— he wants to help and to enable them to fly on their own.

- Possesses the courage to accept that she may not be recognized externally for victories that she experiences internally.

- Re-defines success as the change he can make in his organization and in the world around him rather than by the change and advancement that others can enable in his rank and status.

- Holds faith and trust that, in the long run, doing what is right and just will work out best for everyone.

- Lives under the philosophy that investing in her own personal gain is far less impactful than investing in others.

- Recognizes that every day is a choice. The servant leader does not feel a victim to his circumstances or believe that he deserves to be treated differently than those around him. He is defined by his own actions and choices and not by results that are out of his control.

The terms "Servant" and "Leadership" do seem to oppose each other and to create a tension that is uncomfortable and unnatural. The resolution of this tension, however, is the root of greatness and requires boldness, risk, and humility. Servant

Leaders are not weak, meek, and passive— they are Rebels with a Cause, sacrificing whatever it takes to drive the greater good of their people, their organization, and the world around them. These servant leaders are critical to establishing a successful culture of empowerment, and embody what is necessary to bring the concepts from this Part of the book to life. So for you *Rebels* out there, go forth with a silent swagger, supercharge your innovation cultures, and "May the Force be With You".

PART III:

DISCOVERING OUR SUPER PURPOSE

"It is not enough to be industrious; so are the ants. What are you industrious about?"
-Henry David Thoreau

"Purpose" is one of those words that evokes a lot of imagery and emotion. It speaks to topics like "the meaning of life" and "making the world a better place". And while having a clear purpose can translate into a more altruistic, spiritual, or philanthropic set of actions, it does not necessarily need to be that profound either. To me, knowing your purpose is to have an appreciation of what you love to do, what you are meant to do, and what impact you can make on the world around you— and then focusing your primary efforts toward turning that understanding into action. It is not enough to be successful but be unfulfilled, to be sprinting but without a finish line, or to be innovating without improving lives. When living your purpose, you should feel personally content, be focused on a clear goal, and see changes to the world around you.

I need to give the disclaimer that as I write these words, the search for true purpose is still a work in progress for me personally. I have seen glimpses of it over the years, but am still actively working to figure it out for myself and to thus fully wrap my life around it. And while my full purpose may still be fuzzy, it is clear that there are elements of creating, teaching, helping, solving problems, and writing. Although I may not know the final answer (if there is a definitive answer), I do realize that I must deliberately dedicate time and effort against these elements, and, of equal importance, I must also de-prioritize other time-consuming activities that take focus away from these areas. Said differently, while it is important to prioritize time and effort against what we *should* do to fulfill our purpose, we must also consciously eliminate tasks and activities that we *could* do if they do not add value or take away from our primary mission. By no means should all hobbies, fun, and frivolities be eliminated from life in favor of a single-minded pursuit of purpose, but rather some hard choices should be made to eliminate non-value added tasks to free up time for the crucial activities. To find fulfillment and to make a super impact on the world, we must know who we are, decide what we are supposed to do, and then go do it.

As you prepare to dive into this last Part of the book, know that this is easily the most divergent and the least structured of the three. I am not about to unveil some sure-fire way to discover one's passion and purpose. Rather with these final chapters I have attempted to provide a series of stories, thought-starters, and examples to help provoke some ideas, evoke some emotions, and hopefully spark an insight or two. There will be the usual suspects of superheroes and movie references with even a fable mixed in. The intent is to help you to hone in on your personal passion and "super" purpose, to uncover some "kryptonite" and obstacles along the way, and to remind you to keep everything in perspective. A passionate sense of purpose can be the key to unleashing super-charged innovation and to unlocking personal fulfillment, driving change in our organizations, in the world, and in ourselves.

21

Life is a Race, but Why are We Running?

Running. I will be honest, I am not a fan. My wife is an outstanding distance runner, and truly enjoys just "going out for a run". Her passion is not driven by winning, succeeding, or a sense of accomplishment— it is truly about a feeling of enjoyment and fulfillment (of course... getting out of the house for awhile, away from me and the kids, probably doesn't hurt either). It is not that she doesn't want to excel in her races— she does have aspirational goals and has received a lot of accolades— but that is not what drives her. She really seems to enjoy lacing up the running shoes, getting out and filling her lungs with the brisk winter air, and driving her legs up and down the Cincinnati hills. Her love for running fuels her, and any success that follows is a bonus... and not the other way around.

For me, if there were a four-letter word to describe my emotion toward running for the sake of running, it would not be "love". Don't get me wrong, I do actually quite enjoy a good run at times, but as a means to an end and not as a joyful event in itself. If I have a ball and am trying to score, if there is a finish line toward which I am racing, or if there is some wild animal chasing me, then I am "all in" to exert myself fully and completely. But the thought of lacing up my old running shoes, contracting my lungs with the icy winter wind, and limping up and down steep inclines around the neighborhood feels more like WORK than it does FUN. If there is an objective or goal to chase then that is what will drive me, and any love or joy will be driven by the success at the end far more so than the act of running in itself.

Our lives and our careers are also a type of race, often more grueling than a 26.2 mile marathon (for most of us, this race will last more than 30 years!). There is always some sort of goal that we are pursuing, whether it be a project milestone, career advancement, the meeting of someone's expectations, or even simply a paycheck. We invest our time, passion, and energy into this race, and we spend more time running through our careers than we do with our families, our friends, and our hobbies. But why? What is our motivation? As we fly through our jobs and our lives, do we truly understand what is motivating us to keep propelling ourselves forward, fast, and furious?

We may race for months, years, or even decades without taking the time to stop and to remember why we started to run in the first place— and whether that same motivation holds true today. Sadly, it is usually something bad that happens, like a monumental failure at work, a funeral of a friend, or a trouble at home that stops us in our tracks and forces some introspection. Most of us have been running for a long time and plan to keep running well into the future, but when push comes to shove, we may not really comprehend WHY. And I am not saying that any one way is better than the other— whether we run primarily for "the love of running", for the accolades of the "win", or for some other reason altogether— all are fine reasons to stay in the race. It is, however, important to understand what our true motivation is, to insure that we are making deliberate choices accordingly, and to know that we are not just running blindly.

WHY DO WE RUN?

Racing for the Finish Line? Is there some goal, deadline, or prize that we are chasing that has a defined course, duration, and finish line? Do we know when to sprint, when to pace ourselves, and when we can accept our "award" and relish the accomplishment?

Chasing a Carrot? Are we chasing a moving target, sprinting toward some "opportunity" not knowing when and if we will actually catch it? Do we know how long we will need to sprint or what we will do if we get tired of running? Do we even like "carrots" enough to continue running when the "award" is uncertain?

Being Chased by a "Ghost"? Rather than running toward a goal are we running away from something or someone? Are we driven by a fear of failure to ourselves, to our missions, or to someone else? Do someone else's expectations or our own outdated demands upon ourselves cause us to run from something irrational and unimportant rather than toward something real and fulfilling?

Stuck on a Treadmill and afraid to Fall Off? Have we been running and running, like a hamster in its wheel, while going nowhere? Are we tired of running but afraid that if we stop that we will fall off and get hurt? Do we enjoy the exercise of the treadmill but yearn to get outside and into a real race?

Everyone Else is Running, and We Don't Want to be Left Behind? Are we surrounded by motivated runners and afraid of "losing"? Does everyone else seem to have a finish line that they are chasing, so we feel like we must chase it too?

Are we searching for internal fulfillment or for external validation from benchmarking versus others?

No Freaking Idea... Just Started Running and Never Stopped? Like the iconic image of Forrest Gump, running from coast-to-coast... have we been running for so long that we have forgotten where we are going or why we started in the first place? Has running just become normal with the assumption that life / results / next steps will just happen naturally along the way?

The Building is On Fire? Is there a sense of danger and panic all around us so we feel the need to run just to survive? Is there a culture of fear and urgency that results in frantic activity? Is there a perception that if we are not running then we must not sufficiently appreciate the "crisis" that we are in?

Need the "Runner's High"? I will talk later about the "Adrenaline Addiction"– are we HOOKED on the excitement and exhilaration that comes from a good, hard run? Does the FIX we get from running keep us going quickly, whether or not we truly need to be moving so fast?

Fulfilling a Perceived Obligation? Are we trying to win the race because we WANT to or rather because we feel like we CAN or SHOULD? Are we trying to live up to either self-inflicted or externally-accepted expectations, and competing so that we have proof that we are the BEST? Are we prioritizing validation from the outside over self-assurance from the inside?

Simply Love to Run? Are we running because we undoubtedly, undeniably, and uncontrollably enjoy it? Are we immune to the expectations of others, the addiction of accomplishment, and the seduction of success, and solely doing what we love, because we love to do it? Does the work itself provide enough joy in itself that we don't need a finish line, a pat on the back, or a medal? Do we run because we want to and not because we have to?

Running through life is inevitable and CAN be a very healthy activity. It is important to maintain an optimal balance of fulfillment in the moment as well as satisfaction in chasing a goal, and that balance will be different for each one of us. Even individually, the scales may sway dramatically over the course of time. If our primary goal in the moment is to get promoted, then we should likely be willing to trade off some fun and choose to work a more grueling schedule. If our top driver is in "enjoying a run for the sake of running", then we can likely choose not to *play the game* and to do less activities out of a sense of obligation and more out of a sense of passion. The important part is not to have a certain correct motivation, but rather to stop running long enough to understand what our true personal objective is, to make choices and commitments to support that objective, and to then chart a course to restart the race. We are going to run, but we shouldn't run blindly or we will end up tired, unfulfilled, and far away from our true finish line. Life is a race, and before we sprint out of the gates we need to understand why we are running.

22

Squandering our Most Precious, Non-Renewable Resource... Time

I do my best to be responsible with resources in my life. I drive a fairly fuel-efficient car, I recycle all of my cans and bottles, and I try to conserve water. For these tangible items, it is fairly easy to make a deliberate choice to be efficient because it is clear that "stuff" can run out. But my most valuable resource, one that is entirely finite and disappearing at a consistent rate, is one that I waste far too often and regularly take for granted. This resource is one that I can largely impact and invest how I best see fit, but that I often incorrectly treat as if it is out of my control. This resource, which is our greatest gift but that disappears forever once used, is Time.

Time management is easily my greatest weakness and an area in which I desperately want to improve. Don't get me wrong— I get a lot done. I have managed to navigate a pretty successful career, to start raising three amazing young kids, and to still achieve some personal accomplishments along the way.

But it isn't pretty. I am blessed to have a high capacity, through a combination of God-given talents, work ethic, and sheer will. I am cursed, however, with a low efficiency, through an over-ambitious nature, poor prioritization, and low discipline for distraction. So while I manage to accomplish a lot, it comes at a price.

That price comes in many forms. There are physical ramifications, such as sleep deprivation, poor exercise and eating habits, and increased anxiety, but the total impact can go far deeper than what shows on the surface. The over-extension that results from a high capacity/low efficiency cocktail can impact my ability to be fully invested as a husband and as a father. By stretching myself too thin and by trying to do too much, I may check more total boxes at work but not allow the time to make sure that the one or two truly important projects get my best attention. Additionally, by always stretching beyond a reasonable means, I am always deficient or behind on something. This can lead to feelings of failure or even depression— despite all of the positive things that might be getting done. And what's worse... this "cocktail" is intoxicating, and it is hard to break this addiction of over-extension once it starts.

In this chapter, I will highlight some of the principles of time management that I have learned over the years. Some of these I successfully practice, some I have tried but have not maintained consistently, and some I have not yet had the discipline to implement.

1) **Set one to three over-arching goals at the beginning of each year and actively prioritize time against them**. This seems like an obvious one, but it is not only critically important but incredibly difficult to do. Why else does almost every New Year's Resolution fail? I had a success here one year when I decided that I wanted to complete a triathlon to help me get back into shape. I didn't own a bike and had never swum

competitively (so why I chose this particular event as a goal is another story in itself!). But I proactively prioritized my time to get this done. I signed up and paid for the triathlon, bought a bike, and blocked off the necessary time on my calendar each week to train and to prepare. I also told several people I was doing it to help make it *real* beyond just a goal in my mind. Essentially, I committed and invested and thus was able to successfully complete my goal that summer in Pittsburgh. However, for this one success I could tell the stories of 10 failures… this takes a lot of discipline and choices, but when done successfully helps to insure that you can do the things that are truly important to you.

2)   Set realistic goals each and every day and be deliberate about not only what you WILL do, but also what you WON'T. Setting big goals for the year is important for the big picture, but doing so each day is what ultimately enables success. Waking up each morning and deciding the tasks that you critically must complete that day is the first step in insuring you address your most important goals. That being said, deciding what you will complete is actually the easy part… it's deciding what you will *not* complete that is the real challenge. For me, I can easily highlight my priorities each day and set out to achieve them. However, I am not good at proactively choosing to <u>not do</u> certain activities, and I thus allow the new events of a given day to distract me from my key goals. I have often gotten to the end of the day wondering how I failed to complete the only task that was truly important. It wasn't the failure to set the right priorities, but rather a failure to have the discipline to avoid things that can get in the way.

3)   Learn to use a big 2-letter word… NO. If you are around small children often, you know that they are the masters of this… "No, No, NO!" rolls easily off their tongues if someone tries to turn their energy from what they want to be doing. But somewhere along the way, we tend to lose either our ability or our license to exercise this concept that we so easily had mastered as children. In the workplace, we often feel so much external or self-inflicted pressure to say "yes" to everything that we take on too many responsibilities... and the truly important ones end up lost in the mix. Simple in concept, but hard in execution, we have to use more 2-letter words to focus on what is really important.

4) Learn to ignore the clutter. This is a big one for me—I have a tendency to put off working on the big things until I can clear some of the smaller, distracting ones out of the way first. For example, "I will put that presentation together as soon as I clear out my email inbox" is something I tell myself in the hope that it will help me focus. The reality is that there never is a time in which the clutter is eliminated and I ultimately end up either compromising the quality of the "big thing" or, more likely, end up giving up an evening at home to address it. There will always be clutter that can't be totally eliminated, so it must be allowed to fade to the background.

5) If you aren't going to add or receive true value from an event... don't go. I could spend every minute of every day attending meetings if I accepted everything that came across my desk. "Let's have a meeting" is commonly the proposal to address an issue, but more than often these meetings fail to produce a solution... often because we jump too quickly to the perceived "action" of a meeting without the forethought of an agenda. I recommend avoiding any meeting that does not have a clear and stated objective— there is very low probability that a meeting without a clear agenda will be a good use of time. And if there is an agenda, I look to determine if there are topics that either require my unique perspective or expertise or will help provide me with knowledge to further my own work. If I am going to be redundant or if I am going to be getting information that may be interesting but ultimately not useful, I try and avoid the meeting and to use the time more productively.

6) **Keep one calendar for your life... not a separate one for work and home.** This is another concept I strongly believe in, but don't effectively practice. There is a lot of talk about work/life balance as if they are two separate things. In reality, in today's world the line between where "work" ends and "life" begins is blurry (if not non-existent). Being connected through iPads, Blackberrys and Computers 24/7 means that we are never truly disconnected from work. And even if we could disconnect, the stresses of work will inherently have an impact at home and vice-versa. I have always tried to keep things separate and the result has been that I have far too often compromised my home life and my family. Work produces a lot more "urgent, but not important" requests that can easily trump "important, but not urgent" items at home. When I have been able to maintain my calendar holistically, it has been far easier to make choices that are better in the long-term rather than defaulting to doing what is best only in the short-term. There isn't "work life" and "home life"- there is just "life", and we should manage our time as such.

7) **Never forget that PERFECT is the enemy of AMAZING.** For the perfectionists out there, this one may hit home more than some of the others. To complete a "masterpiece", the first 80% of the work can take 20% of the time, while the last 20% of the work can take 80% of the time. When we want things to be perfect, investing the time in every last detail does take a lot of extra time. And for the truly important projects, the time can be well worth it. The trouble comes when we treat every project, even the small ones, with the same quest for perfection. If we demand perfection out of ourselves in everything that we do, we are taking a lot of extra time and capacity that could be invested in bigger and more important endeavors. For most things, "good enough" really is good enough and we should stop at the 80/20 principle. This allows us to still get the little things done, but to better invest our time making our big priorities "Amazing".

8) Don't entirely delegate your calendar. Despite the fact that time is our most valuable and precious asset, we often abdicate the responsibility of managing it to someone else. Don't get me wrong, there are an immense amount of benefits in following a good program manager or partnering with an administrative assistant to manage the logistics and details of our complicated schedules. Personally, I have been truly blessed over the years to partner with some amazing people who have been key to my day-to-day survival at work. That being said, while there are a lot benefits at the micro level, we need to maintain ownership at the macro level to insure success. How much time do we want to spend each week on the things that are most important? What time must we hold onto for ourselves no matter what "crises" emerge each week? If we do not own this time for ourselves, then there will always be someone or something that is more than willing to take it and we will lose control of our most treasured resource.

9) It is OK to schedule "spontaneity". This one is counter-intuitive and is another area in which I struggle. While I accept that my life is far busier than I like, I truly value having the time to be spontaneous and to do something exciting and unplanned. On the surface, it sounds ridiculous to "schedule spontaneity", and it feels like an oxymoron. However, at the pace of life today it is becoming increasingly difficult to have time magically open up to do something outside the demands of work and home. Deliberately blocking off some space on our calendar to walk the halls and chat with co-workers, to call a friend or colleague we don't see very often, or to have a night out with a significant other is a way to insure that we make the time to do it. We don't need to pre-program the time and can be spontaneous within that window, but blocking off the time insures that there is even a window at all.

10) Don't answer emails if you don't want to engage further. I once read that for every email you send, you get 8 in return. I don't have any hard data to support that but it feels about right. When I feel like I am making progress in responding to the flood of email, I actually end up creating a typhoon of work for myself. As I look at my emails on a given day, the majority can be considered "information only", can be better answered by someone else on the distribution, or can be easily solved with a 30 second conversation. In these cases, I try to have a "one touch" policy and either file it, forward it, follow-up in person, or do nothing. In all cases, when finished I delete it and forget about it. I reserve my emails for the issues and conversations that can truly benefit from an exchange of data and perspective– often for working issues with individuals and teams outside of my office and/or time zone. Email can become a 24-hour, 7 day/week job if we respond to everything. Be selective, communicate to your teams that you prefer live conversation versus email, and don't be afraid to push "Delete"!

Again, the majority of these are tools that I am aware of and support, but I unfortunately don't consistently practice what I preach. This is my biggest growth area and I am committed to trying to improve and to invest more time in the truly important places in my life. Just taking the time to write this book is in part an effort to make my need for time management "real", and to start making better choices with my time (so I don't, say, write a chapter on time management at two in the morning!). Life, as they say, is short and gets shorter every day. William Penn once said, "Time is what we want most but use worst." Let's take the most precious resource that we have at our disposal, and be deliberate about investing it wisely each and every day.

23

Breaking the Adrenaline Addiction

My name is Mike and I'm a Workaholic. And I am not alone.

A wise former manager of mine once gave me a valuable piece of advice about an internal obstacle that can get in the way of living one's purpose— a lesson which I initially ignored but have since leveraged and repeated countless times over the years. He told me to "Beware the Adrenaline Addiction." When work gets to a frantic level of stress, speed, and excitement, then we learn to survive, and even to thrive, on the adrenaline rush that comes with it. This "drugged up" state becomes the norm, and we can become an "adrenaline junkie". Even though we know that it is self destructive, it has become a habit... and one that is hard to break. Eventually, though, something has to give, and we find ourselves needing to slow down. Whether it is because health issues start to arise, work performance starts to suffer, or family life begins to erode, we find a need to take a step back— to get our priorities in order and to get work back under control.

And while, on the surface, this sounds like a very straightforward decision to make, it does not account for the powerful and lingering effects of the adrenaline addiction. There will be a period of "withdrawal" that occurs, and even as we consciously want to slow down, we find ourselves looking for a "quick fix"– a crisis or late-night presentation that we can throw ourselves into so as to get the rush to which we have become so accustomed. And this effect is not exclusive to individuals. Whole organizations can get so habituated to operating in an almost out-of-control crisis mode that when it is rightfully time to pull out of the crisis, it is extremely difficult to do so. Organizations often continue running in a frenetic, tactical pace long after the crisis has passed, because slowing down and becoming strategic is unnatural and even painful. This adrenaline effect is very real, and the accompanying withdrawal needs to be expected and overcome.

The first several years of my career were spent in a fast-paced downstream innovation environment, littered with one crisis after another and largely focused on fire-fighting. It was a whirlwind, high pressure role that was entirely unpredictable and dynamic. It was extremely intense and highly stressful, and… if I am completely honest with myself it was a lot of fun. As fun as it was though, after several years I started to burn out. While I know that I am built more as a sprinter than a marathoner when it comes to work style, it became clear that in trying to sprint the *career* marathon I was going to run out of gas before the finish line. I was working far too many hours, not leaving myself time for hobbies and activities I loved, and, most importantly, not investing as much time in the central relationships in my life.

Something had to give. So after a lot of debate, I decided to pursue a much more upstream innovation role in the hopes of not only growing my skills and experiences, but to hopefully catch my breath as well. That is not to say that upstream work is easier, less challenging, or less important– in reality, this new role was far more technically complex, creative, and critical to the long-term success of the business. The main difference was that this role was now *proactive* rather than *reactive* as I was focused on building the future rather than on keeping the present from burning down.

As I prepared to start this upstream work, I was excited to take on the new challenge and particularly to now have more time to think, to be strategic, and to create a vision. As I asked my wise manager for advice, he did not talk to me about best practices, technology approaches, or strategic thinking. What he instead cautioned was to "Prepare for the withdrawal effects— they are going to be your biggest challenge." He insisted again and again that this would be a big hurdle, and that I needed to be prepared for it and to resist the urge to "relapse". And while I listened intently, I truthfully thought that he was crazy. The thought of slowing down and growing in depth rather than breadth was exactly what I *wanted*, and I wasn't expecting a case of withdrawal but rather was anticipating a sense of relief!

I couldn't have been more wrong. When the constant flux of requests, accomplishments, and crises were removed from my life, I felt anxious, worthless, and even depressed. The adrenaline rush that had been my constant companion for so many years was now gone, and the sense of withdrawal had a significant impact on my performance (at least my perceived performance), my efficiency, and my overall job satisfaction. While I now had more time to think, plan, and design, both the quality and quantity of my work felt to be decreasing rather than increasing. Adrenaline had been my "performance-enhancing" drug, and it was clear that I had developed an unhealthy addiction to get me through my job. I was an addict and I needed to break the habit.

Ultimately, I did learn some tricks to overcome this (although I am not immune from an occasional relapse), and as a leader I have tried to help coach and guide my organizations to be aware of the signs of adrenaline addiction and the withdrawal effects that can ensue.

Common Signs and Symptoms of Workaholism resulting from Adrenaline Addiction:

You have built up an "overworking" tolerance. It takes more and more time, contributions, and commitments to experience the effect of "job satisfaction".

You work harder and longer to avoid or relieve "withdrawal" symptoms. If you experience a "lull" or go too long without experiencing the "thrill" of an urgent deadline, excessive "overtime", or being stretched beyond capacity then you experience symptoms such as guilt, boredom, or restlessness.

You've lost control over your Workaholism. You often work excessively even though you have promised yourself or your significant others that you wouldn't. You may want to stop over-working, but it is compulsive and you feel powerless.

Your life revolves around your work addiction. You spend your waking hours alternating between obsessing about work and recovering from the toll your addiction takes on you.

You have abandoned activities that you used to enjoy, such as hobbies, sports, and socializing, because of your Workaholism.

You continue to over-work, despite the major problems it causes, such as sleep deprivation, relationship struggles, health concerns, or even depression.

5 Step Program to Overcome the "Addiction"

1) Admit You Have a Problem *and* that You Want to Fix It. Like any form of addiction, until you acknowledge that you have a problem and that you want, or even need, to fix it then no change can be initiated. If the symptoms above resonate strongly with you, then you must actively decide that this is a problem that you want to fix.

2) Get Clear and Deliberate on the 3-5 Things that You Will Actively Do. Look at all the priorities and activities in your job and declare the top 3-5 in which you will invest your time. Be specific. Imagine yourself a year into the future and looking backwards. What are the areas in which you will be proud and in which will be most impactful. Resist the urge to cram several sub-points into your top points (i.e. don't have 3 to 5 priorities each with 3 to 5 more hidden sub-priorities!). You should be able to rattle them off quickly in an elevator speech if needed.

3) Be even more deliberate on 1-2 Things that You Will Actively NOT Do. This step should be painful. In some ways, it is easy to declare what you *will* do. It is, however, far more difficult to declare what you *will stop* doing. Write them down, share them, and keep yourself honest.

4) Take control of your calendar. Schedule Thinking Time, Talking Time, and Downtime for yourself and block it off on the calendar. Treat this time as if you would any other meeting and stick to it. Not only will this slow you down, this time will actually make the rest of the day far more effective and efficient.

5) Invest at least 2 Weeks to Change a Habit. Don't expect an overnight miracle. Commit to making the change and force yourself to tow the line for at least two full weeks. Ideally, find someone else to hold you accountable and help you "get back on the wagon" if you stumble.

Once free from the grips of *addiction*, you will find that you can start doing "Less with More" rather than "More with Less". Your work will become more *instrumental* and not just *incremental*. Your teams and your organization will become stronger as you can further invest in building relationships and making connections. You will find that investing more in yourself and less in your job will actually *increase* your impact at the office. And, most importantly, your health, your relationships, and your overall well-being will increase.

I would love to say that I have completely overcome this *addiction* and that I have mastered a "drug free" life. Unfortunately, I relapse more often than I would like. This "adrenaline effect" is real and the accompanying withdrawal is significant. The trick is in being aware of the signs and in taking action to turn things around before it is too late. I now am much faster to recognize the problem and to catch myself before I go through too long of a self-destructive period. This addiction is a common *kryptonite* that must be overcome to fully realize our super potential. It isn't easy, but is critical in leading a purposeful and happy life both at work and at home.

24

Don't Capture the Moments.
Experience Them.

Have you ever sat in the audience of a small child's dance recital? If you picture the stage, it is one of the cutest, most entertaining events that you will ever witness. There is a colorful explosion of costumes— some that fit really well and some that obviously were made for a child at least a foot taller. Some of the aspiring ballerinas are confident and happy to be on the stage "showing their stuff", while some try to hide and fade into the background. A few of the stars and starlets are so conscious of shining for the crowd that they find center stage, pose, and smile from ear-to ear, while at least one little boy is so oblivious that he stands calmly and proudly with his finger two inches up his nose. It really is quite an experience and one that should be cherished and treasured. Now... picture the same recital but this time instead of looking at the stage, look at the audience. It is beyond comical. Mothers standing awkwardly in the aisle with more camera equipment than most Hollywood film crews. Fathers sitting in the crowds, not watching the stage, but trying to watch their daughters through the 2 inch by 3 inch view screen on their iPhones. Teachers trying to figure out the logistics for taking pictures after the event in a session that takes three times longer than the recital itself. Truly, there often is a far greater production in the audience than there is on the stage.

So why do we do this? Why do we visit something as majestic and awe-inspiring as the Grand Canyon and instead of soaking it all in, we instead fill up our camera's memory cards? Why do we take dozens of pictures of store-bought birthday cakes that we will never look at again? Why do we rush to post our "pride" on a social media site (in 140 characters or less) before we hug our sons and daughters? What is it that we are so afraid of or what are we trying to accomplish? At the end of the day, I believe that we are trying to capture the moment so that someday in the future, when we have more time, we can go back and enjoy it. I think it is a desperate attempt to slow down the crazy pace of life and compensate for the lack of brain space that we have available to process the moment by trying to store it in a mental "external hard drive". This is crazy of course, as there really is no substitute for the moment itself, but it is a compensatory behavior to help us try to find a concrete keepsake from an important event. It is because we fear that we will otherwise lose the moment forever in the tornados of our busy lives and minds. We often let our fear of forgetting an amazing experience lead us to behaviors that do not allow us to actually enjoy the experience itself.

I sometimes am envious of people who lived in the times before all of the technology we have today… when life was slower and there was more time to think, enjoy, and reflect. I sometimes wish that we could throw away our cell phones, laptops, and iPads and spend more time fully engaged in the moment (although, I'd like to keep the modern luxuries of indoor plumbing, grocery stores, and toilet paper). But that is not the world in which we live, so we need to find ways to allow ourselves to fully engage and experience important moments in our lives.

And while the examples above are easily brought to life in the "real world", these issues are at least as big of a presence in the workplace as well. How many meetings have you attended where the team's primary focus was on capturing action items and next steps rather than on contributing to debates and discussions? How often do you attend a meeting where one person is talking or presenting, while the other nine people are investing more energy in their computers and phones than on the meeting itself? How common is it for individuals to attend a team meeting just so that they can check a box and document progress rather than investing the time in actually contributing to progress themselves? This lack of mental investment and commitment and this spirit of capturing follow-ups rather than truly experiencing and participating in debates not only is wildly inefficient but ultimately hinders true innovation. We often feel like our ability to multi-task and to attend a meeting, write a summary, and answer emails— all at the same time— actually makes us more productive because of all of the extra activity that we can capture. In reality, our true contributions are drastically reduced by doing multiple things with partial effort than by focusing on a smaller number of things in which we can fully invest. While we may have a documented "portfolio" of progress, illustrating that we were contributing to many innovation projects, we are not able to truly invest the time in actually driving the big innovation that we seek.

So what can we do differently?

1) Can we spend 95% experiencing and 5% capturing? Whether on vacation or in a meeting, clearly there is still a need and desire to create a snapshot, document, or keepsake to recall the event itself. But we can discipline ourselves to actually first engage in the activity and capture it at the end rather than focusing on capturing something so that you can try to experience it later.

2) Turn off our "capturing" devices and turn on our brains. If we have a camera or computer in our hands, we are going to use it. Keep it in the bag until the event is over, and invest our full selves in the event. Fully engage while in the moment and keep distractions out of sight and out of mind.

3) Be choiceful with your time— do one thing at once. We often feel like we are doing ourselves and our teams a favor by trying to do 3 things at one time. In reality, we are often compromising everything... slowing down all 3 things and actually diminishing the innovative potential of each activity.

Life is moving way too fast and there is often far more to get done than there is time to do it all. It can be overwhelming, and it is easy to feel fear that life is going to pass us by. Benjamin Franklin once said, "You may delay, but time will not, and lost time is never found again." The passage of time is inevitable and no matter how hard we try, all moments will pass us by. We cannot capture a moment, so let's have the discipline to fully invest and experience in the key moments of our lives. Let's allow ourselves the license to sit back and enjoy the full splendor of life's "dance recitals" and worry less about trying to capture them in an album.

25

When the Heroes Feel Like Failures

I started this book by comparing the role of the Innovator to that of a Superhero, saying that our jobs, quite literally, are to create a better future by making the world a better place to live. Whether we are searching for the elusive cure to a devastating illness, are making technological advances to improve how the world learns, communicates, and interacts, or are formulating better consumer products and services to improve day-to-day life, we are all on a mission to leave the world better than when we started. And while I write this book from the perspective of business innovation, this analogy spans, probably even more strongly, to the innovators outside of the "cubicles" who heroically serve as parents, coaches, and teachers— improving the lives of our children, families, and friends each and every day.

This Superhero analogy works for me because I am fortunate to have surrounded myself with amazing people, who accomplish astonishing feats of problem solving, invention, and execution each and every day. As I write this, I want to imagine a certain confidence and swagger as these proud, accomplished individuals saunter through the hallways, reveling in the dragons slain, the "Mission Impossibles" made possible, and the tall buildings leapt with a single bound. I want to feel a culture of endless possibilities, of imminent success, and of fearlessness. I want to see and feel all of this in my mind, but unfortunately the reality is that it is often the exact opposite that holds true.

These very heroes, who accomplish amazing feats and have so much to be proud of, often go home each night feeling more like failures than successes. Instead of focusing on all of the good that they achieve and the obstacles that they overcome, they instead dwell on the boxes that they haven't yet checked and the "To Do List" that seems to grow even faster than a speeding bullet. I am personally experiencing this internal sensation of "failure" even as I sit here and write these pages. Over my past week, I managed to make some dramatic progress on some key business challenges across more topics than my short-attention spanned temperament would typically allow— and yet as I shut down my computer late on Friday evening I was overwhelmed with the weight of what was yet to be done both at work and at home. After a week in which I should have felt "super", I instead felt "defeated" as I dwelled on the problems that I was not able to solve rather than the ones that I conquered.

So how do we as individuals, as leaders, and as mentors help to focus more on our epic successes rather than on our unfinished business?

You Can't Save Every Kitten from a Tree. The reality is that at any given moment, there are more tasks to be completed, emails to be answered, and meetings to be attended than can possibly be achieved, no matter how super your powers are. If you measure yourself by *doing everything* then you have doomed yourself to failure before you even start.

Eliminate or delegate tasks that are low priority, delete emails (don't just ignore them, *Delete* them!) that you know you will never get to, and skip meetings in which you will not add unique value. There will always be kittens in trees, and it is impossible to save them all.

Never Fail to Save the World Because You Are Saving a Kitten. Make sure that you predominantly focus your effort on the "World Changing" and "Hero Worthy" missions that you uniquely are designed to deliver. Find the places where your powers are most suited to make a key business and organizational impact and disproportionately invest your time there. Block it off on the calendar and be deliberate about where you do and do not spend your time. If you delay "saving the world" until all of your mundane chores are done, then the fate of the world is doomed.

Leverage Your Powers and Know Your Weaknesses. Just because you are a superhero does not mean that you have to solve every "super" challenge. If you are Batman, and a mission requires flying and X-ray vision then leave it to Superman rather than abusing yourself in trying to solve something that others are better *suited* to do. There are more than enough problems to go around, and focus your energy against the obstacles in which your unique powers are best utilized. That is not to say to only do "easy" rather than "hard" missions, but rather to avoid your personal *kryptonite* and to focus on areas in which your utility belt is best armed to solve.

Make Sure You Trust the Source of the "Batsignal". A Superhero often will be called in to save the day when a key crisis emerges. And when the "bat signal" is projected into the sky, this hero will drop whatever she is doing and bolt into action. This bias to action is part of what makes the hero "super", however it is critical to know and to trust the person projecting the signal into the sky. There are a lot of real crises but also a lot of manufactured ones. There are a lot of leaders who will only yell "Fire" when the house is burning down and others who yell because they like the excitement of "fire drills". Before answering the call and running to save the day, make sure you know that it is a crisis worthy of your time and your talents.

Don't Neglect Your "Secret Identity". Even the best of superheroes cannot be solving all of the world's problems every minute of every day. Taking time to rest, refresh, and recharge is not a waste of time or a dip in productivity. It is critical to step out of the crisis and to invest in your health, your well-being, and your relationships. Read a book. Watch a movie. Go for a run. Take a nap. Take some time to put your cape in your briefcase, and to enjoy an evening as "Clark Kent". Otherwise, you will burn yourself out and your powers will have run out when you need them the most.

As innovators and as leaders, as parents and as teachers, we are surrounded by an endless barrage of crises, challenges, and obstacles in a world that gets faster and more complicated every day. No matter how talented, how dedicated, or how hard-working we are, we cannot do everything. The world will not end if the email inbox is not emptied or if you miss a meeting. Your kids can live happy lives if the dishes don't get done or the laundry does not get put away. Failing to check every single box does not make you any less of a Superhero, so do not let these small "failures" defeat your sense of accomplishment from the central missions that you complete. Focus your time, your energy, and your powers where they are needed most and take pride in your successes… and trust that some kittens will find their way out of the trees without you.

26

Sabbatical Moments

This past summer, in an effort to be more purposeful in my life and work, I made the choice to take a seven week sabbatical so that I could completely detach from the trials and tribulations of the office. And it was awesome. It was a true *summer vacation*, reminiscent of my own childhood... creating magic and adventures for the four most important people in my life. It was a choice that my wife and I had deliberated and debated for several years, before finally deciding to take the plunge. I will certainly do it again, I would recommend it to anyone, and I am dumbstruck that this choice was ever a difficult one to make in the first place.

I am fortunate that my company offers this policy, in which every five years an employee is eligible to take up to three months of unpaid leave. This really is a nice benefit, but one that ridiculously few employees take advantage of. On the surface, a key reason why many may choose not to sign up is the financial implication. Deciding to go without a paycheck for one to three months is no trivial matter of course— but with some planning and preparation this is a hurdle that can be overcome. And while the dollars and cents might be the most tangible hurdle, they are by no means the biggest one. A second obstacle is fear. Fear of being judged by others, fear of being seen as lazy or undedicated, fear of losing a status or equity that one has built... this fear is as much subconscious as conscious and can certainly stop a sabbatical in its tracks. The third is a loss of perspective to one's true priorities. Clearly a career is important, not only in yielding financial security but also in providing a sense of accomplishment and personal achievement. But is it the most important facet of one's life? If anyone were to ask me my top priority in life, my answer is simple— my family. And while I know this to be true without a doubt, do my actions and the ways in which I invest my time reflect that prioritization? The *muscle memory* of the day to day grind of the office can become so engrained, so automatic, that a decision to reinvest even a small amount of that time back to the family or to another top priority can seem like a radical idea.

So why did I personally choose to take this sabbatical? One of the more fascinating elements of this experience for me was in hearing the theories from friends, coworkers, and curious others as to my motivation. No... I am not sick, disabled, or dying, but thank you for the concern. No... I am not so disgruntled with my career / company / management, that I decided to "make a statement" by taking an extended leave. No... I am not working on my "Plan B", spending my days networking, going on job interviews, writing a screenplay, etc. Again, why must the decision to take a sabbatical be the result of some extraordinary chain of events? I had spent 16 years (192 months!) on the job, so taking one or two off mustn't be so dramatic.

One simple reason I did decide to take the leap was that it just felt like the right time to step away and to take a rest. We all work a lot of hours and expend a lot of mental and physical energy, not just in the office but out of the office as well, and I decided to invest this time now to recharge and refresh. That is one reason but not the main one. The main reason was to give my full and undivided attention to my family and to my kids. Each of my kids is at an age where they still actually want to spend time with me and also still think that I am cool (it's all relative, of course), so I wanted to give them the gift of time. When they said, "Dad, can we do X, Y, or Z today?", I wanted the freedom to just give them a "Yes" without hesitation.

And what did we set out to do? What goals did we strive to accomplish? Nothing. Well, at least "doing" was not the focus of this break... the focus was instead on "being". Being at rest. Being present. Being engaged. Being happy. Being silly. Being free. Don't get me wrong, we were incredibly busy and had an "adventure" each and every day— whether it was camping out in the backyard, learning to water ski on a lake, playing catch at the park, rising early for some fresh donuts, going to an amusement park, etc— but these were not goals to accomplish but rather moments and experiences to share. Our focus was not on "what we do" but rather on "just being".

In sharing this experience, I want to pass on the steps that I took and that I would recommend for anyone setting out to take some time, whether it be months or days, detached from work and invested in life.

7 Steps to a Successful Sabbatical:

1) Grant Yourself Permission. The first and most important step is to give yourself the license to step away. The world will not end. Your team will survive. You ultimately will successfully re-enter the workforce. It is too easy to look at time away from the office as a *cost*. Rather look at it as an *investment* and invest the time in what matters most to you. And not only will this investment pay off at home, but it will in the office as well. Countless studies highlight the benefits of rest and escape on creativity and innovation in the workplace, so an investment in a break from your career will not only have a short term benefit on you, but a long-term one on the work itself.

2)   Clean Your Plate. As amazing as my 7 weeks away from the office turned out to be, the two weeks preceding the sabbatical were some of the most intense of my career. This wasn't necessarily a bad thing, but a deliberate choice to clear my inbox (I actually left with zero messages!), to clear my calendar, and to clear my clutter, so that I could escape with a clear mind. I invested the time in finishing what I needed to finish, but more importantly in setting up my team around me who so graciously stepped up to take on my role as I stepped away.

3)   Let it Go. Once I detached, I stayed detached. I removed my email and calendar from my phone, said good-bye to my co-workers, and disconnected entirely for the 51 days. Of course, there were temptations along the way to check in on a pet project, a critical deadline, or the state of my team. But in choosing to vacate the office, I chose to resist that temptation (which got easier each day) and to fully immerse myself in the sabbatical.

4)   Be... Don't Do. I touched on this earlier, but I chose not to focus this break on accomplishing goals, but on being happy. There were no measurables, success criteria, or checklists... just a daily commitment to have a fun adventure and to enjoy each other's company. And with that philosophy, we not only created a life's memory of experiences but also a *culture* of contentedness and relaxation.

5)   Just Say Yes. In life, particularly with our kids, we have to say "No" a lot. There are so many things to do and there is never enough time to do them all. Once you remove 50+ hours a week of work, there is suddenly more time to say "Yes". Take advantage of it and go off the beaten path, walk the long way, or have that extra scoop of ice cream. This simple three letter word can open more doors and create more innovative experiences than you can imagine.

6) Eat, Drink, and Be Merry. The quest for a healthy mind and soul did not necessitate a quest for a healthy body. This sabbatical was not about conserving and dieting, it was about indulging and celebrating. Have a surprise big meal with family and friends. Have ice cream for breakfast. Enjoy a beer (or two) in the middle of a Tuesday afternoon. This is not gluttony but merely enjoying the little pleasures of life, without guilt, with the people you care about.

7) Stop and Smell the Roses. When taking an extended break, there are inevitably some quiet moments where the world slows down into a tranquil meanderance. Take these moments to reflect on how amazing the big things in life are, and force yourself to laugh at how much of our stress and drama is the result of self-inflicted overreaction to small stuff. This sabbatical helped to remind me how lucky I truly am, to celebrate all that life has given me, and to return to work with a more grounded perspective.

I wrote this not to rub in the fact that I had a seven week vacation (although it was amazing!), but rather to encourage each of you to find **sabbatical moments** in your own lives. Maybe it is an extra long weekend, a night where the usually open computer stays closed, or an impromptu lunch at the park with family or friends. We all work hard and even play hard, and deserve a moment, an evening, or a stolen vacation to relax and to recharge. Steal... no INVEST some time to enjoy the important people and moments in your life, and boldly give yourself a license to rest.

27

The Fable of the Dangling Carrot

Allow me to diverge here for one chapter, both in topic and in format. As we pursue purpose in our careers that will ultimately drive results in our organizations, a lot of energy can be expended in chasing "carrots". Sometimes, this chase is exciting and real and can actually be a motivator to keep us going on our personal quests for satisfaction and for purpose. Other times, this chase is frustrating and artificial and can distract us from the work and the mission that both fulfills us and also allows us to drive winning innovation. The below story is a fable based upon the latter ·quest for a carrot, and the implications that this chase can have on our sense of fulfillment, on our organizational culture, and on our business results.

The Fable of the Dangling Carrot

A long time ago, in a meadow far, far away... there lived three rabbits. They were all happy, hard-working, and ambitious young bunnies who supported themselves and their families by farming lettuce in their three neighboring fields. The rabbits had become good friends and often helped each other so that they could maximize their collective success. Their boss was a sly, old fox who was quite happy with the rabbit's results, but wondered if there were ways that he could *motivate* them to work even harder. The fox was rather perplexed about how best to do this as he had nothing tangible to offer the rabbits, but he was greedy to grow his business so he set off to devise a plan.

The fox locked himself in his burrow for several days, brainstorming, ideating, and deep-diving before finally he had a scheme that he thought just might work. So the next morning he went to the meadow, called the three rabbits into a meeting, and began to unveil his plan. "You all have done a masterful job of building our lettuce business," said the fox, "and I have been quite happy with your success." The rabbits all smiled proudly, looking around at the lettuce fields that they had grown. "However…" said the fox, "the times are changing and we need to step-change our progress and to grow more lettuce than ever before!" The rabbits gave him their full attention and anxiously awaited the brilliant vision from the fox. The fox proclaimed, "If we are truly successful then one or more of you will have the opportunity to leave these lettuce fields and to gain a more prestigious role, to bring in more *green* for your families, and to even supervise some rabbits of your own." The fox then pulled a juicy, orange carrot from his pocket and dangled it in front of the bunnies, whose eyes and mouths were now widely gaping.

"If you can seize this challenge, work even harder, and achieve breakthrough results, then you may have the opportunity to farm carrots like these instead of that boring, old lettuce… and only then will you experience unprecedented success and glory." The first bunny exclaimed, "Wow! I want those carrots! How much progress must I make?" The second bunny blurted, "That is amazing! When will we know who has succeeded?" And the third bunny, looking intrigued but more skeptical, asked, "What's the catch?" The fox, expecting these questions, calmly explained, "There is no catch... you have my word that there are carrots on the horizon. I can't give you specifics on *when* or *how many*, as the future is very uncertain, but I can say that the harder that you work, the better your chances." With that, the first two bunnies ran to their fields and began working while the third bunny went off to find a quiet place to think. And the fox walked away, feeling confident that his plan had succeeded.

What the racing rabbits did not realize, however, was that when the fox dangled that carrot, there was no carrot field yet to be found. The fox wanted to be in the carrot business, and hoped that he could deliver on his proclamation, but had no tangible carrot to offer. He decided to sit back and wait to see how the rabbits responded before planning his next move.

Back at the meadow, the first rabbit had built a fence around his field and was working alone harder and faster than ever before. The second rabbit had chosen not to seclude himself from the others and continued to work during the day as usual. However, every night he left his family and went back to the field to work alone through the night. The third rabbit chose not to change his behavior, but rather to keep doing what had been successful in the past. However, because the rabbits were no longer working together, it had become harder and less fulfilling to deliver the same results.

After the first year, the fox came back, carrying the juicy dangling carrot, to assess the rabbits' results. He entered into the first rabbit's fence and was pleased to see that the lettuce field was noticeably bigger and more fruitful than ever before. The rabbit looked tired, but proud of what he had done. When the fox went to the second field, the rabbit was not yet there but was running from his home looking dismayed. The fox was pleased to see the progress, but the bunny looked distracted and desperate that he had done enough to earn the carrot that the fox still held. At the third field, the rabbit stood, content with his work, which was not a dramatic improvement from the previous year but consistently strong. The fox shook his head in disapproval, and went on to praise the first two rabbits. "I am quite pleased," said the fox, "and clearly you have been working hard to reach our goals." "Unfortunately," he stated slowly, "there is no carrot field to be awarded this year... but if you keep up the good work then maybe next year will be the year!" The third bunny shrugged and went back to his field, the second bunny had tears in his eyes as he sulked back toward his house, while the first bunny looked angry but determined as he hopped quickly back inside his fence. Each went back to work in their respective fields, determined to earn the elusive carrot from the fox.

Another year passed, and when it came time for the "carrot dangling" the fox was almost giddy as he pranced back to the rabbits' fields. He could not wait to see how much that they had accomplished, and to figure out how much richer he would become. However, as he approached the fields he started to become suspicious that his plan was not working like he had thought. As he approached the first bunny's fence, the bunny rushed up to meet him and began taking the fox through an extensive presentation about why he, and not the other two bunnies, deserved the carrot. He had elaborate charts, drawings, and graphs on his fence wall and spoke extensively about his personal merits (and the flaws of the other rabbits!). It was an impressive display, but the rabbit talked for so long that the fox did not even have time to look behind the fence to see the results. As he walked to the second rabbit, he could see the dark circles under the bunny's eyes and a look of pleading upon his face. The bunny pulled out his timecard and showed how many extra hours that he had invested, how many nights he had spent in the field, and how hard it had been to be away from his family for so long. The fox gave him an encouraging pat on the back, tried to look empathetic, and thanked him for his work. He then slipped away and went over to the third bunny's field. The third bunny barely looked up from his work as the fox approached. The fox surveyed the field and saw the consistent results that he had grown to expect, but was surprised by the bunny's general lack of interest.

He engaged the third bunny in conversation, who told the fox, "I know that you're probably pleased with the short-term results that we've all achieved, but I am concerned about the long-term implications. One bunny is so concerned with the prestige of earning his carrot that he is neglecting his actual work and relationships to invest more time in 'campaigning'. The other is spending so much time away from his family that I am worried about his health and well-being. And for me... the culture just is not very collaborative anymore and it is no longer fun for me to work in the fields." The fox looked shocked at these words and also at the third rabbit's questioning of the fox's own masterful plan. He gave a disapproving stare to the bunny and then went to address them all. "Brilliant work and strong results for each and every one of you", said the fox. "I am pleased by your progress and optimistic about our future." "However... while our results are good, they are not good enough and I am sorry to inform you that there are no carrots to be awarded this year", the fox said slowly and carefully. He waited, as the rabbits' reaction clearly showed their frustration and disappointment before saying, "But I am optimistic that next year just might be the Year of the Carrot!"

The fox then quickly left the fields to go back to his burrow and to count his profits. He was still quite pleased with how his plan was proceeding, but was beginning to worry about the third bunny's words of caution. The fox knew that he would eventually need to come through on his carrot promise, but decided to wait one more year and to further line his pockets before finding a way to award the carrot.

At the time of the third year's review, the fox went back to the fields. He tried to remain optimistic as to what he would find, but had a lingering doubt in the back of his mind. And as he approached the first bunny's field, his doubt was rapidly turning into concern. He saw that the fence was higher, that the graphs and charts were more extensive, and that the bunny was ready for another profound presentation to impress the fox. It was clear that this bunny was no longer on speaking terms with the other two bunnies and that he had become obsessed with nothing but winning the carrot. The fox stopped the bunny before the "sales pitch" could start and instead went inside the fence. The fox has shocked and dismayed to see that both the quantity and the quality of the lettuce field had deteriorated rapidly! Clearly the bunny had focused on style over substance, and the results had suffered dramatically. Anxiously, the fox hurried out of the fence (with the first bunny hopping behind him still trying to deliver his rehearsed presentation) and went to the second bunny's field. The bunny looked much more content and healthy than the previous years, and told the fox, "You may notice that my field is smaller this year. The quality is still high, but I decided that I needed to spend more time with my family and less time in the fields. I had become so obsessed with the carrot that I was neglecting my family…. and I realized that carrots weren't really that important to me anyways." The fox was glad to see the high quality, but dismayed to see yet another decrease in production. He went over to the third field and again saw the consistent, steady growth that he had grown to expect… but the third bunny was nowhere to be found. He saw a note from the bunny that said, "Dear Fox, Thank you for the opportunity and I apologize for the short notice. I have decided to leave this job and to go to work for myself growing my own lettuce. I wish you luck and please send my best regards to the other two bunnies. May you all solve the dilemma of the dangling carrot."

The fox was floored and dismayed by what had happened, and shocked by the failure of his plan. He hurried back to his burrow (when he finally evaded the first bunny who was still unceasingly continuing his pitch), to deal with the realization of the situation. Now... not only were there no carrots in the horizon, but there was no longer enough lettuce either. He looked onto his table at the carrot that he had been dangling, and what had once looked bright and promising now looked cold and depressing. That very carrot, which had once tantalized and entranced the bunnies, now just teased and mocked him. The fox tossed the carrot in the trash and sat wondering how his leadership of the bunnies had gone so wrong. He then saw a turnip on his shelf and had a new, brilliant idea...

The Moral of the Story:

For the Bunnies: Before our purpose becomes the chase of a carrot, we must make sure that 1) we even like carrots, 2) the carrots are real, and 3) we understand the costs of the chase.

For the Fox: As managers, we must not dangle a carrot unless we can deliver, otherwise we will create a culture where our *bunnies* will become disgruntled, distracted, and disappearing... and we will become a leader with no followers.

28

It's Just Soap

A few years back, my good friend and his family stopped and visited our home in Cincinnati after a long weekend in Boston. They were heading home after the fateful events of the 2013 Boston Marathon. He is an amazing runner and had finished the race well before the tragic bombing that ultimately killed and injured far too many racers and bystanders. And although he had crossed the finish line with an outstanding time, he actually walked away somewhat disappointed because he hadn't quite met his ultimate goal... narrowly missing a personal best time. He and his family were already in their car heading back to the hotel with the race behind them, when the text messages he was receiving changed from "Congratulations!" to "Are you OK?" In that moment, suddenly all of the past preparation, the mix of excitement and disappointment of finishing, and the future planning for the next race went from critically important to utterly trivial. The result of the race no longer mattered as the now meaningless matter of "Win or Lose" was replaced with the sobering realities of "Life or Death".

I often think about the runners who were on the verge of finishing when the bombing took place. Months if not years of training, the labor of 26 miles behind them, and suddenly they are quite literally knocked off their feet. What do you do? Do you get up and finish the race? Do you stop right away and help those around you? Do you realize that it ultimately does not truly matter whether you cross the finish line or not?

Our projects and our jobs are often like training for a marathon. We invest countless hours as well as blood, sweat, and tears in trying to make an impact for consumers, for our organizations, and on our personal careers. We take pride in our work and are passionate about what we do, and this passion is often a key driver in our ultimate success and satisfaction. But even if we are driven by this passion and highly invested in our missions at work, we have to remain pragmatic. No matter how important, urgent, or intense we believe our jobs to be, we have to remember that it is just work... and that there are far more important things in life (that if we are not careful, might knock us off our feet).

1)   It is Just Soap! My teams over the years have been tasked with developing breakthrough Beauty Care products, such as deodorants, body washes, and shampoos. It never fails to amaze me how much insight, creativity, and technical depth goes into innovating, improving, and inventing products such as these that virtually everyone uses but largely takes for granted. While I know that my teams are making a difference for the business and for consumers around the world, I encourage each individual to always keep everything in perspective. While it is important and amazing to have passion for the job, it is critical to remember... It is Just Soap. That is not to say that our careers should not be an important focus in our lives as they absolutely should be. We spend 40+ hours each and every week working, so we should strive to find something rewarding and fulfilling. The problem arises if our careers actually BECOME our lives. If this happens, we will not only see our personal lives suffer, but will see our job performance negatively impacted as well.

2) You are not your project. Passion is an important element in innovation, and, in almost every case, a person who feels a personal connection to his project will experience greater success. Passion yields commitment, commitment yields investment, and investment yields results. However, like most strengths, if taken too far a weakness will emerge. An extreme passion can lead to a case where the project goes beyond being the product of one's efforts to being an extension of one's self. In essence, the person goes past taking pride in the fruits of his labors and begins measuring his own worth by the results of the work. We must invest ourselves in delivering a product of worth, but not define our worth by the product that we deliver. Your work is what you do... it is not who you are.

3) Whatever the issue, it is not LITERALLY "life or death". How often at work are you faced with a problem presented as some form of "This presentation must go well because the fate of mankind is at stake!"? Now unless you are a heart surgeon, police officer, or special agent Jack Bauer, whatever challenge you face in concept is likely nowhere near as intense in reality. As human beings, I believe that we have an innate desire to feel important and to accomplish something meaningful. And with that desire, we (or those around us) can amplify a molehill-sized issue into a mountain of a problem to fulfill that unconscious desire. At times, we can take a simple "go or no go" decision and make it seem like "life or death". This is not to say that we should not treat issues seriously. Just not *too* seriously.

4) Emotion can overwhelm judgment. An over-investment in the work can not only have a detrimental impact on the individual, but also on the work itself. An excess emotional attachment to a program can lead to an over-reaction toward a conflicting management decision, a confrontational approach to opposing points of views, or an irrational fear of bad results or the "death" of the project. It also can taint the lens through which we study and evaluate data, and we might see only information that supports our point of view while avoiding that which is contradictory. When passion makes pragmatism difficult, it is important to set clear success criteria, to force data-based decisions, and to partner with a trusted team, peer, or mentor to keep you honest and to check your "blind spots".

5)   Consider the "5 Year Rule". When presented with a stressful situation, I like to ask myself, "Will I remember this 5 years from now?" For the vast majority of situations, the answer to this question is a resounding "No". At the very least, answering this question helps to keep things in perspective and to dial the stress level down a few notches. Often, this helps to make decisions about how best to invest my time. Do I invest my discretionary time in putting out a series of small fires, or in building the foundation for something amazing? Do I spend my afternoon answering the constant barrage of emails or investing in supporting and growing my team? Am I consistently prioritizing the urgent and trivial activities over the programs and relationships truly important in the long-term? Am I confusing the urgent for the important? Clearly it is impossible to apply this rule on each and every occasion as life is full of "small stuff" that we inevitably need to "sweat". But we do need to be deliberate and decisive in managing our calendars and our choices to insure that we are not consumed by the forgettable daily grind and that we invest time each and every day in building programs and relationships that will be memorable into the future.

6)   Never forget "Rule Number 6". One of my favorite speakers is Benjamin Zander, Conductor of the Boston Philharmonic, Teacher at the New England Conservatory of Music, and Author of "The Art of Possibility". Zander tells a story of two prime ministers sitting in a room, when suddenly the door bursts open. A man rushes in, extremely upset, shouting, and carrying on. The resident prime minister says, "Peter, Peter, please remember Rule #6." Immediately Peter was restored to complete calm. Soon thereafter, a young woman comes in, hysterical, shouting, and out of control. The resident prime minister again said, "Please remember Rule #6!" Immediately Maria said, "Oh, I'm so sorry," and she apologized and walked out. This same thing happened a third time and this time the visiting prime minister said, "My dear colleague, I've seen three people come into the room in a state of uncontrollable fury, and they walked out completely calmly. Would you be willing to share this Rule #6?" The resident prime minister smiled and said, "Oh yes, Rule #6 is very simple. DON'T TAKE YOURSELF SO DAMNED SERIOUSLY." And so the other man said, "Oh, that's a wonderful rule. May I ask what the other rules are?" And the first man says... "There aren't any other rules." I love this story and the reminder to not take our jobs and our lives too seriously. (And the irony is not lost on me that I am taking myself too seriously by having 5 other rules preceding this one...)

Again, this is not to contradict the whole premise of this Part of the book by suggesting that passion for a career is bad. It is, in fact, a critical element not only to job satisfaction but to overall life fulfillment as well. The key is to find balance and to keep it all in perspective, especially knowing that at any moment we might get knocked off our feet. There is a great quote by Rabbi Harold Kushner that states, "Nobody on their deathbed has ever said 'I wish I had spent more time at the office'." We need to find the right balance of passion and pragmatism, keep the perspective that our life's purpose is bigger than our jobs, and always remember that we are working to live and not living to work.

29

Business Travel by Mega-Bus and Other First-World Problems

Over the course of my career, I have traveled the world. With domestic travel to virtually every major metropolitan area in the United States, and international travel around Europe, South America, and Asia, I have racked up frequent flier miles and hoarded hotel points. With the benefit of a global company, generous travel budgets, and aggressive research plans, I have filled my passport while enjoying the comforts of business class flights and accommodations. Don't get me wrong, it is hard work and difficult to be away from my family... but I have at least *struggled in style.*

The times have changed, however, and as budgets have gotten tighter so have the travel options. Things were so tight one year that I could not find the money in December for a quick in-an-out flight to Chicago for a meeting. To be fair, this was not a meeting that I *had* to attend, but rather one that I *wanted* to prioritize, so the travel restriction in this case was justified. But still, I wasn't willing to give up, so I started searching for a Plan B. I could have just driven to Chicago from Cincinnati— it is a 5-hour drive and I actually kind of enjoy the peace and quiet of a long stretch of uninterrupted highway cruising. But I was so swamped at work (I'll come back to that), and was not willing to spend 10 round trip hours behind the wheel when I could have been working. So I then looked into the Megabus. For about $20 bucks, I could secure a round-trip ticket on a 6-plus hour double-decker ride. The ride had heat, Wi-Fi, and a scenic route through rural Indiana, so I bought a last-minute ticket and started the adventure. "Plan B" in this case stood for "Bus".

The other issue with taking a bus versus a plane was that I could not do the trip in one day, so I also had to find a hotel room on a dime. I took to Priceline.com and searched for the cheapest name-brand hotel that I could find, that was walking distance from the bus stop and had at least a couple of stars in the rating. And while it wasn't the lap of luxury, I did find a respectable place that met my criteria (i.e. cheap), booked it, and started on my way.

The night of my trip, much like most of that polar-freaking-vortex of a winter, was cold... really, really cold. My sister-in-law was kind enough to drop me off at the outdoor bus stop where for 30-minutes I shivered and waited for my *stagecoach* to arrive. There was only one other traveler waiting with me— an *interesting*, young fellow who was embarking on a 4-day, 4-state trip to follow the Cincinnati Reds caravan, an event where several of the team's players visit various cities across the Midwest meeting fans and signing autographs. He had no luggage, no money, and no place to stay, and had decided to keep warm by spending the 3-hours prior to the bus ride drinking the last of his dollars in a bar. We had the same conversation a couple of times (which he won't remember), until finally the bus arrived. Interesting, yes... First Class-y, not so much.

When I climbed the stairs to the top of the bus, I was surprised to find it empty. I was very relieved by this as I could spread out, plug in my computer, and spend the next 6 hours "building the business" with email, one-pagers, and presentations. Looking back, it really was not a bad set up. I had space, I had time, and I had the world wide web. In that particular moment, however, I was less able to see the "big picture". I was uncomfortable, I was cold (then hot, then cold, then hot), and I was tired. And the work itself was as tiresome as the ride. This wasn't the fun, innovative, strategic work that I love to do, but rather the drudgery of busy work, petty email arguments, and politics that I had put off as long as I could. By the time I finally had arrived in Chicago at 1:00 the next morning, I was feeling pretty sorry for myself.

I limped off the bus, threw my bag over my shoulder, and asked Siri to help me get my bearings so that I could start the half-mile walk to my hotel. It was even colder in Chicago, and I wanted nothing more than to find my "cheap" hotel and a warm bed. While walking and staring intently at the map on my smartphone, I only vaguely heard a strong, yet tired voice asking me for help. An older, homeless woman stood shivering in front of me, asking for bus fare. She was clearly freezing in the frigid wind chills, so I pulled out my wallet and gave her a couple of bucks without a thought or a word. After walking about half of a block, I realized that, not surprisingly, Siri had led me the wrong direction so I grew further annoyed and doubled-back toward where I now believed the hotel to be. Shortly thereafter, I again came across the same woman, who was now waiting for a bus. She looked at me with sympathy and asked, "Are you lost?" I smiled and politely said, "No", and explained that I was on the right track for my hotel. She then started walking with me and said, "Don't worry. I will help you find it." I politely refused a couple of times, but she was determined to keep walking and so we started the cold walk together in the snow.

Along the way we talked about Chicago, about the weather, and about other random topics that came to mind. I offered again to go on my own, but she said that she was happy to "keep movin' and be stayin' warm" so she continued to walk. When we finally could see the hotel sign in the distance, she pointed it out, made sure I knew the right path, and started to go on her way. I asked her if she had anyplace warm to go, and she said that she just planned to try to stay on buses as long as she could until the morning when warm, public places start to open their doors. I asked if there was anything that I could do to help, and she said that there was a place nearby that she could stay— "not nearly as nice as the fancy place that I was staying" (and silently griping about) — but that it was $15 and far too much to ask. I gave her a twenty, she gave me a hug, and we both went our respective ways.

So, why am I telling this story? It is not to highlight my own philanthropic performance— to be honest, I would sadly have probably ignorantly paid no attention to the woman if I had not been so directionally-challenged in the city. I am telling this story as a reminder to keep things in perspective. On a given day, I can find myself overwhelmed with "problems"— a mountain of emails that I need to climb, political games played by co-workers to make minor issues seem major, and "life-or-death" crises that must be resolved urgently so that the "fate of the business does not crumble around us." In reality, there is nothing that we do or don't do that will bring on the end of the world.

And the ironic thing is that it is not the mountains in life that cause most of the stress— it is the molehills. When there is a true crisis, a real problem that needs to be addressed, a person in need who requires a few dollars to survive in the cold, then we are able to focus, to put all of the *crap* aside, and to work together to solve a problem. It is the minor day-to-day issues— the petty arguments around an artificial deadline, the posturing for credit or promotion, the complaining about taking the bus versus taking a plane that create most of the conflict, time, and stress. If we were able to keep things in perspective and to let the mountains be mountains and the molehills be molehills... if we could focus on what was truly important not just in times of crisis, but in times of peace... if we would remember that even our worst possible day in the office is pretty darn good in the whole scheme of things, then we could find more tranquility, satisfaction, and fulfillment as we all co-exist together in this crazy world.

We live in busy and stressful times, and the workplace often reflects and even exaggerates that atmosphere. It is easy to get caught up in the frantic panic-of-the-day rather than to stay grounded on what is truly important. Every day is a choice. If those around us turn molehills into mountains, we don't have to climb them. And we can pour our energy and focus into what really matters. God placed this woman in my path on the cold streets of Chicago as a reminder to hold on to the "big picture" perspective and to not let the trivialities become overwhelming, and so I am paying this story forward onto you.

30

The "It's a Wonderful Life" Effect

Purpose. I close out this Part of the book, having walked through many of the obstacles, dangling carrots, and psychological traps that get in the way of living a purpose-driven career. For me, I am 16 years into a successful career and I still find myself spending a lot of time reflecting on "what I want to be when I grow up". It is not that I am unhappy or even dissatisfied. It is just that I sometimes am overcome by a nagging feeling that something is missing... that there is more that I could be and should be doing. Now, I'm not saying that I need to quit my job and enroll in the coast guard, start an orphanage, or join the circus. All of these may be worthwhile endeavors (although I have no concept of what my circus act might be), but I don't *necessarily* need to do something that drastic. What I am saying is that I want to be more deliberate going forward with how I take the talents, interests, and experiences that I possess and invest them into the world around me. While that could of course require a significant career change, it could also mean optimizing my time in my current career, or supplementing my "day job" with activities where I can utilize my interests. For example, I have had a strong desire to write a book for as long as I can remember, but was never able to find (i.e. make) the time for this commitment. While I can't commit to quitting my job and fully investing in this endeavor (bills to pay, mouths to feed, etc.), I was able to invest at least some time in pursuing the interest and that, in fact, is how the three-year inconsistent adventure of writing this book was born. And here I now sit, writing the final chapter.

Still, I personally am in the process of figuring out 1) what is the "purpose" for which I was made to serve, 2) where are there opportunities for me to better invest my time in serving that purpose, and 3) what choices must I make to pursue said opportunities? Essentially, how do I start now and deliberately choose the right path forward? If as you read this, you feel a similar nagging or yearning, here are some final thoughts that I personally am using as I "work on purpose":

To know where you're going, you have to know where you've been. While I am a big proponent of living in the moment and aiming for the future, I believe it is critical to reflect on and to extract insights from our past. This is not about "those who ignore their history are doomed to repeat it", but rather about understanding the experiences, talents, and successes of the past so that you *deliberately can* repeat it. What are the times in your life that made you the most proud? What talents do you enjoy and have invested your time in growing and nurturing? What experiences have had a profound impact on your life and how can you share those with others? What daydreams have you consistently had that have not yet been brought to reality? Take some time to map out the areas of life that have truly made you proud, inspired, and successful and compare that with where you are today. What elements of the past have you let fade away and how can you bring those back into your present and future?

Understand your "It's a Wonderful Life" Effect. First, if you haven't seen the movie, "It's a Wonderful Life", you should stop reading and go watch this film. Without getting into all the details, the premise centers on a desperate man, George Bailey, who is at the end of his rope. He has reached a crossroads in life where he feels as if he has failed to live up to his potential and that his future is hopeless. George is actually contemplating taking his own life, when he is visited by his "guardian angel" who gives him an amazing gift— the gift to see how the world would be different had he never been born. He sees all of the lives that he would *not* have changed, the fortunes that he would *not* have improved, and the happiness that he would *not* have created. In essence, George Bailey was able to see the unique impact that he alone had brought to the world and gained a new understanding of his purpose in life. As you look back on your life and on your career, don't just look at your "results" from your participation— think about how different the world would be had you uniquely *not* been a part of it. What value to the projects, organizations, and individuals did you add that exclusively exist because of your presence? And even more importantly, as you look forward, what are the areas in which you can make a unique contribution and disproportionately put your energy toward as opposed to places that largely would be the same if someone were to do them. What has your "It's a Wonderful Life Effect" been so far, and how do you want that script to read in the future?

Be hot or be cold, but don't be lukewarm. One of my favorite biblical verses essentially says to not waste time with mediocrity— Either be "all in" or "all out", but don't just meander through life in the middle. As you go to work every day, do you feel inspired or do you feel like you are settling? Do you feel like you are growing or are you coasting? Are you making a difference or simply making do? Now, this is not to say that every minute of every day should be awe-inspiring— it is still work. And on a day-to-day basis there will still, for most of us, be some less than thrilling responsibilities to which we must attend. But in the big picture, are you excited about the mission that you are pursuing or are you just surviving from paycheck to paycheck? In the moment, it is easy to be tempted by comfort, safety, and security. To quote C.S. Lewis from "The Screwtape Letters", "Indeed the safest road to hell is the gradual one — the gentle slope, soft underfoot, without sudden turnings, without milestones, without signposts." Figure out what amazing purpose that you have been designed uniquely to do and pursue it. Get in the game, or find a new game— don't get to the end regretting spending all your time on the sidelines wondering what might have been.

What intentions currently are keeping you from your purpose? This sounds simple enough— so what might be stopping you from working against your purpose? Ask yourself these questions: 1) If money were no object, what would you do? 2) If status were no object, what would you do? 3) If your perceived expectations of the significant others in your life (parents, spouse, siblings, friends) were no object, what would you do? It happens far too often in life that we make choices to do what we deem is responsible or is expected of us and neglect the choices that might truly make us happy. To be fair, often there are real and significant obstacles that exist once you have started down life's path, such as financial obligations, dependent relationships, and security. However, sometimes we make these obstacles bigger than they really are. Is the "extra" money that you make actually buying happiness or merely buying stuff? Are the evenings you invest in striving for a future promotion worth sacrificing your hobbies and interests in the present? Does all of the time and effort preparing for an eventual retirement cause you to miss out on enjoying life today? When all is said and done, how you invest your time is a choice— if you don't feel like you are truly living your purpose today, what are the choices you can make tomorrow to take even a small step in the right direction?

Look for open doors and walk through them.
Opportunity knocks more often than we realize. If you look
back on the major milestones of your life and career, how many
of them had an element of serendipity about them? For
example, during the spring of my junior year of college I was
looking forward to a summer on campus doing research and
teaching chemistry classes (not to mention all the other perks
of living on a college campus). I happened to get invited to a
lunch with a member of the Board of Trustees who wanted to
meet some students studying science and engineering. I
honestly put little thought into the meeting and was not overly
excited about going... but I was in college and, hey, "free
lunch". I ended up sitting next to the Board Member (who it
turns out was the Chief Technology Officer at a large,
innovative company in Cincinnati), had a great conversation,
and ultimately gave him a resume. Two months later, I was an
intern at this company and 16 years later I remain there today.
What are the "free lunches" you pass up because you are too
busy or too focused on the crisis of the day? A professor in
business school once advised that at least once a year we all
should do an extensive career search just to see if a perfect job
is out there. Best case, you find your dream job and live happily
ever after. Worst case, you realize that where you are today is
actually the best place for you. Opportunity knocks often, but
will only meet you if you are willing to open the door.

Some of you may be in a place already where your work and
your purpose are already one in the same— that is truly an
amazing place to be and I encourage you to share your stories.
For others, you may be looking for subtle or even drastic
changes to more deliberately pursue your passions and interests
to make a broader impact on the world around you. This is a
call to reflect on what that purpose might be and to make
active choices to pursue it, even if just with one small first step.
Don't choose a path for your career and your life by chance or
by accident... choose it on purpose.

CLOSING CREDITS:
Agents of CHANGE

"It's kind of fun to do the impossible"

-Walt Disney

As I reach the end of this book, I think it is worth re-asking, "Why did I choose to write this in the first place?"

Clearly part of the reason is a personal passion. Having been in the innovation business for most of my adult life, I had a strong desire to stop and to capture what I have learned up to this point. Team that with my renewed joy of writing and the completion of this book is a logical step. That definitely is a reason but not the biggest one.

A second reason, in all honesty, is a search for personal "Purpose". In running through life, I have had the good fortune to accomplish some fantastic things, to travel to some incredible places, and to meet countless amazing people. While the journey has been positive, it has been haphazard... and I am ready to create a clearer vision for my ultimate destination. Writing this book has been a nice grounding on my philosophies and also on what is most important to me, and I hope that this is a springboard as I start the "second half" of my life and career.

The main reason, though, why I chose to write this book is because I want to help other innovative spirits to find their passion and to reach their potential. Even if only through one small insight or one baby step in the right direction, I hope that the stories, parables, and thoughts in this book might help others to find some focus and direction. I know so many "super" people with limitless power and potential— hungry to change the world, but frustrated by being lost on where to start. I also see a world full of problems to be solved, discoveries to be made, and mysteries to be unlocked, and I know that if these superheroes could be unleashed against the super challenges that more people could find fulfillment while making a purposeful impact on the world.

In my opening remarks, I promised a messy and divergent collection of insights, parables, and principles to help trigger how we can create and drive magical innovation back into our products, our organizations, our careers, and even our lives. If nothing else, I am fairly confident that I delivered on the "messy" and "divergent" part. Innovation is messy, as is life, and as we move forward I truly do not believe that there is some cookie cutter 12-step process to sort everything out. Yet while I don't think that the chaos of the world can be contained, I do think that there are clear, even if highly philosophical, "powers" that we can apply to improve the innovation in our careers and in our lives. If we unleash these powers, then I am confident that we can find personal fulfillment, drive better innovation, and improve lives (others and our own).

In the title of this book, I wrote **CHANGE** to be an acronym, and have yet to define it. "CHANGE" is about **Creating Holistically Amazing New Game-changing Experiences**– not just at work but in our lives and in our world. As innovators, we are the modern day superheroes with the power to transform the world and to improve lives. Be bold, Unleash your Potential, and Be an Agent of CHANGE.

APPENDIX:

50 INSPIRATIONAL QUOTES ON LEADERSHIP AND INNOVATION

Over the course of my career and in writing this book, I have become a collector of quotes that can serve as inspiration in innovation, leadership, and even in day-to-day life. A simple insight— the distilling of a complex situation into a short and pithy concept and phrase is a powerful tool in understanding the world, our teams, and ourselves. So below are 50 (+1) of my favorite quotes from individuals far more insightful than myself...

----

1) "If I had asked people what they wanted they would have said faster horses."

Henry Ford

2) "You can design and create and build the most wonderful place in the world. But it takes people to make the dream a reality."

Walt Disney

3) "Good Is The Enemy Of Great."

Jim Collins

4) "At the beginning of a change, the patriot is a scarce man, and brave, and hated, and scorned. When his cause succeeds, the timid join him, for then it costs nothing to be a patriot."

Mark Twain

5) "If we knew what we were doing, it wouldn't be called research."

Albert Einstein

6) "There are no rules here. We're trying to accomplish something."

Thomas Edison

7) "We more frequently fail to face the right problem than fail to solve the problem we face."

Unknown

8) "Any intelligent fool can make things bigger, more complex, and more violent. It takes a touch of genius- and a lot of courage- to move in the opposite direction."

Albert Einstein

9) "Only those who dare to fail greatly, achieve greatly."

John F. Kennedy

10) "It is said an eastern monarch once charged his wise men to invent a sentence, to be ever in view, and which should be true and appropriate in all times and situations. They presented him with the words, '***and this too shall pass away.***' how much it expresses. How chastening in the hour of pride. How consoling in the depths of affliction."

Abraham Lincoln

11) "Vision without action is daydream. Action without vision is nightmare."

Japanese Proverb

12) "You have to find something that you love enough to be able to take risks."

George Lucas

13) "It is not enough to do your best. You must know what to do, and then do your best.

W. Edwards Deming

14) "If you want to build a ship, don't drum up people together to collect wood and don't assign them tasks and work, but rather teach them to long for the endless immensity of the sea."

Antoine De St. Exupery

15) "When everything seems to be going against you, remember that the airplane takes off against the wind, not with it."

Henry Ford

16) "Imagination is more important than knowledge."

Albert Einstein

17) "Many of life's failures are people who did not realize how close they were to success when they gave up."

Thomas Edison

18) "Some see things as they are and ask why. Others dream things that never were and ask why not."

George Bernard Shaw

19) "There are only two rules for being successful. One, figure out exactly what you want to do, and two, do it."

Mario Cuomo

20) "To avoid criticism- do nothing, say nothing, be nothing."

Elbert Hubbard

21) "Whether you think you can or think you can't, you're right."

Henry Ford

22) "To be yourself in a world that is constantly trying to make you something else is the greatest accomplishment."

Ralph Waldo Emerson

23) "Great spirits have always encountered violent opposition from mediocre minds."

Albert Einstein

24) "I am an optimist. It does not seem too much use being anything else."

Winston Churchill

25) "Managers help people see themselves as they are; Leaders help people to see themselves better than they are."

Jim Rohn

26) "Never doubt that a small group of citizens can change the world. Indeed, it is the only thing that ever has."

Margaret Mead

27) "If you're not failing every now and again, it's a sign you're not doing anything very innovative."

Woody Allen

28) "Good thoughts are no better than good dreams, unless they be executed!"

Ralph Waldo Emerson

29) "In real life, unlike in Shakespeare, the sweetness of the rose depends upon the name it bears. Things are not only what they are. They are, in very important respects, what they seem to be."

Hubert Humphrey

30) "The important thing is this: to be able at any moment to sacrifice what we are for what we could become."

Charles Du Bos

31) "When one door closes another door opens, but we so often look so long and so regretfully upon the closed door that we do not see the ones which open for us."

Alexander Graham Bell

32) "There is more to life than increasing its speed."

Mahatma Gandhi

33) "They may forget what you said, but they will never forget how you made them feel."

Carl W. Buechner

34) "Don't sell your story, just tell your story."

J.J. Abrams

35) "To do great work, a man must be very idle as well as very industrious."

Samuel Butler

36) "There are two possible outcomes- if the result confirms the hypothesis, then you've made a discovery. If the result is contrary to the hypothesis, then you've made a discovery."

Enrico Fermi

37) "I am a man of principle, and one of my basic principles is flexibility."

Everett Dirkson

38) "Only those who risk going too far can possibly find out how far they can go."

T.S. Eliot

39) "Everything should be made as simple as possible but not simpler."

Albert Einstein

40) "Reasonable people adapt themselves to the world. Unreasonable people attempt to adapt the world to themselves. All progress, therefore, depends on unreasonable people."

George Bernard Shaw

41) "There is nothing so useless as doing efficiently that which should not be done at all."

Peter Drucker

42) "You sort of start thinking anything's possible if you've got enough nerve."

J.K. Rowling

43) "You can do anything, but not everything."

David Allen

44) "I have not failed. I've just found 10,000 ways that won't work."

Thomas Edison

45) "The difficulty is not so much in developing new ideas as in escaping from old ones."

John Maynard Keynes

46) "The best executive is the one who has sense enough to pick good men to do what he wants done, and self-restraint enough to keep from meddling with them while they do it."

Theodore Roosevelt

47) "Things which matter most must never be at the mercy of things which matter least."

Johann Wolfgang Von Goethe

48) "What counts can't always be counted; what can be counted doesn't always count."

Albert Einstein

49) "It is impossible to live without failing at something, unless you live so cautiously that you might as well not have lived at all, in which case you have failed by default."

J.K. Rowling

50) "It's kind of fun to do the impossible"

Walt Disney

+1) "Always be yourself, and always strive to be a better person."

Disha Nanda

ACKNOWLEDGMENTS

I wish that I could personally thank each and every individual who has contributed to the creation and completion of this book. Countless co-workers, colleagues and mentors around the world, as well as friends and family members throughout the 39 years of my life have all played a part in the experiences, the ideas, and the examples contained within.

Particularly, I would like to thank the following individuals for their inspiration, their encouragement, and their time in enabling this book to transform from an idea into a reality:

o To my friend and colleague, Veronica Torres-Rivera, thank you for volunteering your time, your creativity, and your brilliant mind to provide a comprehensive final round of editing... focusing less on minimizing errors and more on maximizing the overall holistic design and experience. You have encouraged me more than you know to write, to dream, and to design, and your influence is stamped heavily across these pages.

o To my brother, Jim Thomas, thank you for not only providing thematic and design inspiration, but also for being a tough and honest critic. You helped me to make some of the necessary but challenging changes, and helped me to see some of my "quirks" and "bad habits" as I wrote.

ABOUT THE AUTHOR

Mike Thomas has been in the "Innovation" business for over 16 years, and has had the opportunity to design and deliver new products for a diverse collection of people around the world. He also is a father of 3 super kids, a coach, and an avid movie buff, and works to infuse an innovative spirit at home as well as at work. *Agents of CHANGE* is his first published book, and represents a compilation of the insights, events, and people that have shaped his life and ignited his passion to write.

96058876R00105

Made in the USA
Lexington, KY
16 August 2018